LEADING YOUR SCHOOL TOWARD

EQUITY

ASCD MEMBER BOOK

Many ASCD members received this book as a
member benefit upon its initial release.

Learn more at: **www.ascd.org/memberbooks**

LEADING YOUR SCHOOL TOWARD
EQUITY

A Practical Framework
for Walking the Talk

DWAYNE CHISM

Arlington, Virginia USA

2800 Shirlington Road, Suite 1001 • Arlington, VA 22206 USA
Phone: 800-933-2723 or 703-578-9600 • Fax: 703-575-5400
Website: www.ascd.org • Email: member@ascd.org
Author guidelines: www.ascd.org/write

Penny Reinart, *Chief Impact Officer*; Genny Ostertag, *Managing Director, Book Acquisitions & Editing*; Julie Houtz, *Director, Book Editing*; Katie Martin, *Editor*; Thomas Lytle, *Creative Director*; Donald Ely, *Art Director*; Georgia Park, *Senior Graphic Designer*; Valerie Younkin, *Senior Production Designer*; Kelly Marshall, *Production Manager*; Shajuan Martin, *E-Publishing Specialist*

PAPERBACK ISBN: 978-1-4166-3136-1   ASCD product #123003
PDF E-BOOK ISBN: 978-1-4166-3137-8; see Books in Print for other formats.
Quantity discounts are available: email programteam@ascd.org or call 800-933-2723, ext. 5773, or 703-575-5773. For desk copies, go to www.ascd.org/deskcopy.

ASCD Member Book No. FY22-9 (Aug 22 P). ASCD Member Books mail to Premium (P), Select (S), and Institutional Plus (I+) members on this schedule: Jan, PSI+; Feb, P; Apr, PSI+; May, P; Jul, PSI+; Aug, P; Sep, PSI+; Nov, PSI+; Dec, P. For current details on membership, see www.ascd.org/membership.

Library of Congress Cataloging-in-Publication Data
Names: Chism, Dwayne T., author.
Title: Leading your school toward equity : a practical framework for walking the talk / Dwyane Chism.
Description: Arlington, Virginia USA : ASCD, [2022] | Includes bibliographical references and index.
Identifiers: LCCN 2022011016 (print) | LCCN 2022011017 (ebook) | ISBN 9781416631361 (paperback) | ISBN 9781416631378 (pdf)
Subjects: LCSH: Educational equalization—United States. | Educational leadership—United States. | Educational change—United States.
Classification: LCC LC213.2 .C475 2022 (print) | LCC LC213.2 (ebook) | DDC 379.2/60973—dc23/eng/20220606
LC record available at https://lccn.loc.gov/2022011016
LC ebook record available at https://lccn.loc.gov/2022011017

31 30 29 28 27 26 25 24 23 22   1 2 3 4 5 6 7 8 9 10 11 12

Leading Your School Toward
EQUITY

A Practical Framework for Walking the Talk

Introduction
A Reflection on Education

"Not everything that is faced can be changed,
but nothing can be changed until it is faced."

—James Baldwin

It's state testing day. The 6th grade teachers and students are in the cafeteria, going over the time constraints and expectations for taking the reading portion of the Iowa Test of Basic Skills. Among them is an 11-year-old Black boy, anxiously waiting to begin his test. Once the teachers have gone over the instructions, they ask for any questions and then deliver the fatal last words: "Good luck!"

The boy has his approach planned. He begins flipping through the testing booklet, searching for the shortest passages to read and respond to first. A sense of learned helplessness tells him that he is different from the other students, and his environment has taught him that success depends on completing the test on time.

Forty-five minutes pass. Students are putting down their pencils, having filled in the last of the multiple-choice response bubbles. Each time the boy hears a pencil drop, an internal voice reminds him that he's not as smart as the white kids. In an effort to silence that voice, he grabs hold of another strategy he's relied on before: *when in doubt, choose* C.

This book, *Leading Your School Toward Equity,* is 40 years in the making. My thoughts and ideas around race and equity began to form the minute I walked through the school doors to start my journey in education. As early as kindergarten, I encountered questions about why my skin was brown and began to realize I was not like my classmates. During learning time, I thought my brain was more challenged than the brains of white students, and this was affirmed each time the teacher praised their quick thinking when responding to her questions.

I was that 11-year-old Black boy sitting in the cafeteria, and I was anxious during that test, and most tests, because I was afraid of being exposed academically. My strategy of choosing *C* was undoubtedly flawed. But when I reflect on my experiences in education, I find myself in an awkward space mentally. If it were not for the education I received, I wouldn't be where I am today. Yet, although I've earned a doctoral degree and experienced success professionally, the residual effects of the systemic conditions I faced as a student remain with me to this day.

Looking back, I'm not going to claim that any of the numerous teachers I had were racist. I also believe that most of them had good intentions. What I *will* attest to is that my skin color had an immense effect on my educational experience. It contributed to the opportunities that were available or unavailable to me; to the types of relationships I formed; and to a self-consciousness propelled by the threat of being stereotyped. Despite the asserted purpose of schools to support the learning of all, watching the daily experiences of students who did and did not look like me taught me that equity is not a given. For me, getting an education was more about survival than the joy of learning. And my ability to learn was often handicapped by a desire to hide my deficiencies from peers and teachers.

In looking at the current landscape in education, I believe I'm one of the lucky ones. So many students of color struggle today to overcome the negative effects of having to endure systemic challenges associated with race.

A Purposeful Path to Disrupting Inequity

Although I have found renewed hope in the resurgent interest in equitable education, I fear that the notion of *doing equity* may become the new wolf in sheep's clothing—"nice" ways to evade the deeper-rooted issues and long-standing problems related to racial bias. Much like educators' attempts with No Child Left Behind, Race to the Top, or Every Student Succeeds, adopting an equity focus doesn't guarantee the desired result. Unless we commit to taking bold action, our attempts at equity will simply impersonate genuine responsiveness to demands for improvement and ultimately maintain the status quo (Parish & Arends, 1983).

Because traditional educational systems have failed to bring about the type of institutional reform that dismantles policies and practices resulting in discrimination, it's incumbent on today's leaders to find transformative ways to meet the educational needs of all students. Although there are many books that focus on building teachers' cultural competency, I wrote this book specifically to guide district, school, and teacher leaders in forming an equity-driven culture. Ultimately, classroom teachers' success in meeting the demands of equity depends on competent individuals leading change.

Of course, the focus on school-based leadership does not excuse local school boards and other forms of higher bureaucracy from reimagining policies and practices to support students of color. I have seen for myself the continual pressure school leaders feel to produce equitable outcomes in learning, even as they are forced to operate within larger systems that continue to permit and promote practices that persistently marginalize groups.

However, the hour for change is upon us. Policies need to shift, and school leaders cannot afford to wait for the cavalry. They must be catalysts for change, bringing transformation to their circles of influence. They must courageously deny appeals for "softer" approaches to equity that are driven by a one-culture narrative and seemingly designed more to avoid tension and blame than to build a better educational system that truly serves all.

I wrote this book to help leaders chart a purposeful path toward equity. Leaders will learn how to help their staff both acknowledge *and* address conditions that promote racial inequality. In light of recent discussions regarding social injustice and the need for antiracism (Kendi, 2019; Reynolds & Kendi, 2020), my approach to achieving equity involves securing a force of *educational equity allies*—educators who interrupt practices that incubate intolerance within their learning spaces. These educators persistently educate themselves about the manifestation of racial injustice within their environment, use their position to prevent students from being oppressed, and take explicit action to educate others. If you dare push your organization to confront racial inequality, this book will support you as you develop such allies.

Although much of this book acknowledges the plight of Black students in our schools, the ideas apply to all disparaged groups. I focus on Black students here to acknowledge that across the United States, they face harsher conditions than others within our schools. But rest assured, this book guides leaders to act in ways that enable all students to better connect to the classroom, teacher, and educational system. In the words of Maya Angelou, "I speak to the Black experience, but I am always talking about the human condition."

Educators should see this book not only as a guide to uncover the root causes of educational disparities but also as a tool to disrupt oppressive environments. Reaching a state of equity will require a well-strategized plan, and this book—and its accompanying sets of downloadable resources (handouts at www.ascd.org/EquityLeadershipHandouts and the Appendix's tools at www.ascd.org/EquityLeadershipToolset)—will help you build that plan. But know that this is not a one-time process; it's a continual and an intentional way in which to walk.

A Courageous Journey

Thank you for setting off on this journey. Seeking to lead for equity requires boldness and a willingness to shake and shift school culture. However, leaders who dare to take this step are rightfully wary of what they will be facing. As Radd and colleagues (2021) write, "It is easy to get trapped by fear of others' backlash when you take a stand for greater equity" (p. 29). Fear is a given; it's how we choose to *respond* to that fear that defines our character.

As an analogy, consider stepping into a crowded elevator. The door slowly closes, and what happens next? Most of us will behave in fairly predictable ways: We remain silent, avoid making eye contact, shift our gaze to the ceiling or the floor, or consult our watch or cell phone. It's a little 30-second experience, and yet it's a powerful image of what commonly happens when we sense that everyone's personal space has been invaded and we don't want to appear threatening.

Engaging in equity work will begin much like this elevator experience. The moment someone drops the word *race*, awkwardness is injected into the environment. Some people in the room will become silent, avoid making eye contact, avoid conversation, start looking up, start looking down, or consult their watch or cell phone. Some people will want to get off the topic of race as quickly as some want to get off that elevator. They may fear the vulnerability such conversations bring. They may fear saying or doing something that will offend. Of course, it's also possible that some may quickly become annoyed and openly express their opposition to continuing the conversation. School leaders can't let any of these factors—awkwardness, trepidation, or hostility—dissuade them from guiding others to challenge the conditions that propagate racial bias, segregation, and harm. It's essential to push forward despite any impulse of avoidance generated by fear.

Before you start down this road, turn the page and take the assessment shown in Figure I.1. It will help you gauge your baseline knowledge and comfort levels in leading others through conversations about inequality and racism. When you have completed reading this book, and after you have engaged in the suggested activities and reflected on your learning, I'll ask you to retake the very same assessment to document how you have grown as an equity leader. Ultimately, success with this journey will come down to one thing—courageous leadership—and that requires going far beyond the motions of just "doing equity."

FIGURE I.1
Leading for Equity: A Pre-Assessment

I am comfortable having conversations about conditions of inequality or racism.	☐ Strongly Disagree ☐ Disagree ☐ Neutral ☐ Agree ☐ Strongly Agree
I am comfortable taking the lead in guiding others through conversations that seek to build their awareness around conditions of inequality or racism.	☐ Strongly Disagree ☐ Disagree ☐ Neutral ☐ Agree ☐ Strongly Agree
I am comfortable delivering truthful coaching and feedback to support others in identifying and addressing instructional practices that are culturally unresponsive.	☐ Strongly Disagree ☐ Disagree ☐ Neutral ☐ Agree ☐ Strongly Agree
I am comfortable with my ability to help others gain the skills necessary to effectively advocate for equity when seeing daily circumstances associated with racial overtones.	☐ Strongly Disagree ☐ Disagree ☐ Neutral ☐ Agree ☐ Strongly Agree
I am comfortable leading others in using data to disrupt racial inequities in my building or district and to establish sound strategies for improvement.	☐ Strongly Disagree ☐ Disagree ☐ Neutral ☐ Agree ☐ Strongly Agree
I am comfortable with my ability to self-reflect regularly to uncover any hidden biases and stereotypes I may possess.	☐ Strongly Disagree ☐ Disagree ☐ Neutral ☐ Agree ☐ Strongly Agree
I am comfortable with my level of understanding around what signifies equity to effectively guide others within my school or district environment in understanding.	☐ Strongly Disagree ☐ Disagree ☐ Neutral ☐ Agree ☐ Strongly Agree
I am comfortable with my ability to provide a sense of value and belief within staff that leads to greater outcomes for marginalized students.	☐ Strongly Disagree ☐ Disagree ☐ Neutral ☐ Agree ☐ Strongly Agree
I am comfortable with my ability to routinely step outside myself to learn how my present reality influenced by race compares with the reality of others.	☐ Strongly Disagree ☐ Disagree ☐ Neutral ☐ Agree ☐ Strongly Agree

1

Paving the Way

"We are responsible for our own ignorance or, with time and openhearted enlightenment, our own wisdom."

—Isabel Wilkerson

While I was giving a presentation to a room full of K–12 leaders, I asked them to take out a piece of paper and engage in a quick quiz. "Using the race groups *white, nonwhite Hispanic, Black,* and *Asian,*" I began, "numerically rank those groups according to where you believe each would fall in terms of academic achievement data. Do this first in reading and then in math."

Having conducted this exercise in multiple settings over the years, I was confident of the results. They would unanimously rank Black students at the bottom, with Hispanic students sitting directly above; there would be mixed reviews regarding which group—Asian or white students—would sit at the top. And that is exactly what they did this time, too. I then asked the attendees what we could learn about equity and race from this exercise, once again accurately predicting how they would respond. Bodies shifted uncomfortably, with attendees either unsure of the answer or uncertain of how to talk openly about the obvious. I let them off the hook and shared the following: *This exercise is a stark reminder of the current reality concerning equity and race in many of our schools. Race, or skin tone, continues to be an indicator of educational outcomes.*

Although we maintain that our schools are institutions designed to open doors and create pathways to a bright and promising future, the odds continue to be unfavorably stacked against students of color. As Smith and colleagues (2017) point out, "Few would disagree with the statement that a child's last name, skin color, or family income should never determine his or her future. But the systems and operational structures in schools and classrooms can do just that" (p. 72). Former Secretary of Education Arne Duncan expressed a similar thought, noting that "the undeniable truth is that the everyday educational experience for too many students of color violates the principle of equity at the heart of the American promise" (Lewis, 2012, para. 5).

The simple explanation for these inequities often includes a narrative of poverty, uninvolved parents, limited exposure to a variety of experiences, or lack of resources. These factors certainly play a role in the educational trials faced by children living in such circumstances. What they cannot explain, however, is why the racial achievement gap continues to exist among students even when they share similar socioeconomic backgrounds and go to the same schools (Reardon, 2016). There must be something more.

The Hunt for Equity

For schools across the United States, the continuous school improvement process serves as a crucial lever in reaching equity and generating student success. However, the standard process of diagnosing the data, creating a plan, implementing the plan, monitoring progress, and increasing activity has not solved this problem. Schools spend vast amounts of time engaging staff in advancing various strategies, only to find that achievement data continue to reveal gaps in opportunity and learning for our most vulnerable population—students of color.

I want to be clear: The intention of the school improvement process is not in itself a roadblock to equity. The problem resides in approaches that work against improvement efforts. Here are some of them:

- **Protecting staff morale.** Seeking to keep the peace often translates into using softer approaches while working with staff on continuous improvement. To keep adults happy, schools may attempt to build a positive culture by focusing on what's going well, overlooking crucial deficits.

- **Focusing on compliance.** Schools may overemphasize the actions, forms, or tasks that staff need to complete but pay little attention to how things are done or the relevance of the strategies selected.
- **Living in the wrong "circle."** School improvement efforts can be halted by focusing on what Stephen Covey (1989) refers to as the *circle of concern*. The circle of concern encompasses areas beyond the control of the school, such as a student's home life. Choosing to focus on outside factors distracts attention from more crucial issues that are within the school's purview.
- **Failing to promote data literacy**. Staff members need to understand how to use data to uncover root causes and identify promising practices. If schools don't spend adequate time building data literacy, stakeholders will be unable to track genuine progress in current conditions. Data illiteracy often translates into distrust in data.
- **Focusing on *all students*.** Schools may avoid addressing or acknowledging disparaging differences among demographic groups, such as ignoring disparities in suspension data to instead address *all* student suspensions. The misguided assumption is that the same strategies affect all students equally.
- **Laying the blame on students.** Schools may see students as the problem and solution to continuous improvement. In this view, students need to change for school climate to change. Therefore, strategies and conversations ignore how adult actions contribute to student experiences.

Effort: It's Not Enough

Let's look at a school that demonstrated a few of these common tendencies when implementing the continuous school improvement process.

Terry, a fifth-year middle school principal in an urban school district, worked with his staff on responding to trend data indicating a disproportionality in suspensions and academic achievement regarding students of color; the latter represented approximately 48 percent of the student population. Terry noticed that office referrals of Black male students were higher than that of the general population. He also observed that teachers were routinely sending minority students to the office for "disrespectful behavior" when they were not sending nonminority students who displayed the same or similar behavior.

Teachers in the building voiced their frustration with minority students in the following ways: "We're doing the best we can under the circumstances"; "Our Black male students are not always focused or motivated to learn"; "Many of our Black students struggle with showing respect to one another and to staff"; and "It's hard to hold our Black students accountable when they aren't held to the same expectations and don't receive the necessary academic support from home."

As part of his multiyear improvement plan, Terry guided staff in looking at subgroup data to determine specific areas of concern and agree on action steps. During the first two years, the staff focused on improving students' buildingwide behavior. Staff members felt that a repaired student culture would lead to increased academic outcomes for minority students. Because this approach resulted in only small changes in behavior and stagnant academic growth, the staff decided to focus on interactions with students and instructional practices that specifically spoke to diverse learners. As a result, they looked to culturally responsive schooling and restorative practices to meet the academic and social-emotional needs of their diverse population.

At the end of the fifth year, the data in Terry's building indicated some success but fell short of the goals the school had set out to attain. Overall, student discipline issues had decreased, but a racial disparity in student suspensions continued. Academic data showed a similar trend; although achievement increased overall, there were minimal gains in closing the achievement gap. Staff members felt the culture as a whole was improving, but they were frustrated that the data didn't reward the effort they were putting in. Terry also noticed improvement within the culture and with teacher practices, but he was frustrated, too. He needed to find more effective ways to influence and energize staff in response to the data.

Coherence and Adherence: The Way Forward

I have seen this challenge to achieve equity mirrored in multiple experiences I've had as a teacher, principal, principal supervisor, and coach. Terry and his staff worked hard during those five years, but the results were nevertheless discouraging. So why did the gains not match their efforts?

The missing piece was coherence. Although Terry and his staff were moving in the direction of equity, they fixated on actions instead of on creating a sound structure that would support a deep awareness of equity. Coherence, according to Fullan and Quinn (2016), consists of a common depth of understanding (individual and collective) about the purpose and nature of the work, the key phrase here being *depth of understanding*. Equity remains elusive in schools when there is no robust organizational understanding among staff members about why equity is needed and how to genuinely obtain it. This requires a larger cycle of inquiry. Although actions and initiatives alone often succeed in creating better conditions for all students, they typically fall short in demonstrating better outcomes for students of color (Gregory et al., 2018; Hollie, 2012).

Nevertheless, there's hope for leaders like Terry. Every student can succeed if we commit to the right practices over time. *Leading Your School Toward Equity* speaks to how leaders and schools can create the conditions that will enable continuous improvement initiatives to thrive. Figure 1.1 shows the four-step Equity Leadership Framework that will guide this work:

1. **Define and clarify equity.** Leaders craft a systematic approach that builds consensus around a standard definition and vision of equity. Everyone comes to understand why the work is so crucial.
2. **Create discomfort.** Leaders promote intentional and continual dialogue about equity and race. They monitor the influence of these conversations, even when they're challenging to hold.
3. **Build efficacy.** Leaders establish a unified culture where adults possess high levels of individual and collective efficacy. Again, everyone needs to be on the same page about effectively educating students of color. If they're not, it can set back the culture.
4. **Normalize action.** Leaders operationalize action inside classrooms and throughout the school. They focus on the actions needed to create consistent, sustained success over time.

As the framework shows, leaders are at the heart of implementation. Realizing equity calls for sound leadership that models what Lee J. Colan and Julie Davis-Colan (2013) refer to as *adherence*, which is the ability to consistently execute. According to Colan and Davis-Colan, consistency in execution requires *focus, competence,* and *passion* from leadership. In the upcoming chapters, we will be looking at ways to build a solid foundation of practice in the key areas of the Equity Leadership Framework, with a central theme of shaping leadership actions that demonstrate adherence. To this end, leadership actions should

- Align with the nature and scope of the work (focus);
- Demonstrate the knowledge and wherewithal to lead the work (competence); and
- Display the obligation and desire to do what is right in the face of inequity (passion).

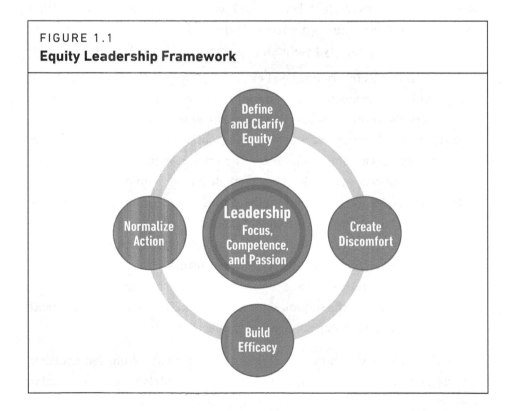

FIGURE 1.1
Equity Leadership Framework

The goal of each upcoming chapter is to empower schools to break the cycle of inequality. As Chip and Dan Heath (2010) note, "Ultimately, all change efforts boil down to the same mission: Can you get people to start behaving in a new way?" (p. 4). Failure to demonstrate adherence will cause the culture to abort strategy and rally around maintaining the status quo. Because the role of leadership is so crucial to success, each chapter concludes with a section titled "Next Steps for Leaders." This not only calls attention to the importance of leadership, but also gives leaders the opportunity to reflect on how they might demonstrate the focus, competence, and passion needed to effectively guide equity work.

LEADERSHIP TIP

Along this journey, you will experience times when you feel mentally exhausted, but mental exhaustion is not an indication that it's time to abandon the work. On the contrary. Push through these moments. Remind yourself often of the moral imperative you are carrying out. Whether you're in an urban setting with a racially diverse population or a rural setting with little to no racial diversity, all educators should take this journey. All students deserve educators who are attuned to the racial aspects of equity and who can craft optimal learning experiences that prepare them to be advocates for all forms of justice in society (Pate, 2020). Just as important, although your environment may not have racial diversity today, you never know where you might be tomorrow. Keep fighting the good fight.

Making the Most of Time

As a former building leader myself, I understand that one of the biggest enemies to continuous school improvement efforts is time. I also recognize that in the world of education, there's never *enough* time, so success comes down to how educators prioritize or strategically use the time they have.

The Equity Leadership Framework is not simply another idea to add to a long list of things you have already tried. This framework develops coherence around the work we should and *must* be doing to change the game for students who are fighting against predictable outcomes. This is not to exclude other strategies that you're currently engaged in, but this work does demand a cohesive mentality around equity that must come first. The Equity Leadership Framework is about the daily way in which staff should walk.

Next Steps for Leaders: Commit to the Work

Actions speak louder than words. Achieving equity will take more than just words. Commit to taking the necessary actions to provide an environment that remains in tune with the experiences of those who come from various backgrounds and conditions. This means building a level of coherence that eradicates blinders constructed around race (Delpit, 1995). Because you are the leading factor in creating and sustaining environmental change, the commitment starts with you.

Ask yourself...
- What are my tendencies when approaching school improvement?
- To what extent do I have clarity of purpose around the work of equity?
- As a leader, how do I exhibit focus, competence, and passion?

2

Defining and Clarifying Equity

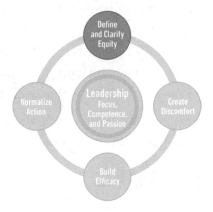

*"Treating different things the same can generate as much
inequality as treating the same things different."*

—Kimberlé Crenshaw

In the absence of coherence around the term *equity,* educators will struggle to recognize how they may be contributing to a system that maintains
*in*equality (Ladson-Billings & Tate, 1995). When equity remains undefined
or only vaguely understood in an organization, focusing on it tends to build a
culture of opposition. Partly this stems from a general resistance to change,
but it's compounded by confusion about why the change is necessary or
whether the proposed alterations to familiar practices will be worth the
disruption. When adults are obliged to construct their own interpretation of
what equity is, there's no uniformity in discerning the conditions and essential actions that support an equity-focused culture.

Let's consider an example that illustrates this challenge. An urban school district had refocused its efforts on achieving equity in each of its schools. As part of this process, principal supervisors were charged with visiting all school buildings to get a baseline of where each building stood. On entering one of the elementary schools, the supervisor was greeted by a banner touting the school's vision for equity. It read as follows: "We are dedicated to ensuring an equitable learning environment for every student, family, and staff member regardless of background." One would assume that this building's leaders had taken measures to define equity for all of the stakeholders. However, working alongside the principal, the supervisor discovered that this wasn't the case. So the supervisor coached the principal in gathering informal data on what staff members thought the school's equity statement meant. Here are some of the interpretations that came back:

- **1st grade teacher:** "It means that I am committed to doing whatever it takes to work with all students and families, regardless of where they come from."
- **2nd grade teacher:** "I believe we can live out this statement by making sure that each school in our district offers the same resources to students as some of our more affluent schools."
- **4th grade teacher:** "To me, this statement means I need to keep high expectations for all students."
- **6th grade teacher:** "I think this means that all students have the right to learn and that it's our job to protect that right."

As you can see, the lack of clarity within the equity statement creates a fundamental challenge: staff do not understand how the school is trying to achieve equity and what role they must play. The 2nd grade teacher seems to think the statement calls for a universal approach to equity because she advocates for similar conditions and experiences for all students. But similarities alone don't guarantee equity. Although the other teachers quoted appear to recognize that they have a role to play in achieving equity, none of them identify any actionable steps that they are taking. The teachers seem to lack certainty regarding concrete actions that promote equity.

Why Define Equity?

The undeniable symptoms of racial segregation in our schools indicate that we need to understand this situation more fully. To borrow a phrase from the authors of *Learning to Improve* (Byrk et al., 2015), educators have a tendency to suffer from *solutionitis,* "a form of groupthink in which a set of shared beliefs results in an incomplete analysis of the problem to be addressed and fuller consideration of potential problem-solving alternatives" (p. 24). This condition is perpetuated when dominant monocultural narratives fail to drum up the attention needed to address inequities. In other words, if we are to reach equity, we must have conversations that build a robust understanding of how we define equity, how we create it, and how it operates within the school.

Building and sustaining coherence around the meaning of equity are ever-evolving processes (Fullan & Quinn, 2016) that must engage stakeholders in developing a working definition of equity. The definition must be operational—seen as functioning within the stakeholders' own setting. This means that building-based actions to pursue equity are in tune with words on equity statements and that the adults frequently revisit established beliefs to provide true accountability. It's imperative to move beyond nonfunctional statements and definitions that offer no investment or fail to deliver a return.

To illustrate the consequences of a nonfunctional definition of equity, let's revisit the urban school principal from the scenario at the beginning of this chapter. After taking some time to reflect on what he heard from select staff, the principal decided to assess why his teachers were not more unified in their understanding of the equity statement's intent. So he sent a survey to staff with a single open-ended question—*How do you feel about our equity statement?*—and solicited their honest (and anonymous) feedback. Several comments clearly indicated that the equity statement wasn't working:

- "I feel the statement hasn't been communicated clearly."
- "I don't think all staff care."
- "The statement doesn't align with decisions that are made."
- "The culture in our building doesn't reflect these words."

Conversely, when a working definition of equity *is* established, stakeholders are aware of conditions of inequity; feel accountable (both individually and collectively); and embrace opportunities for action. In other words, written statements must inspire a cohesive mentality leading to disciplined people, disciplined thought, and disciplined action (Collins, 2001):

- **Disciplined people:** Adults are consistent in diligently assessing and monitoring educational experiences through a lens of equity.
- **Disciplined thought:** These adults are laser-focused on establishing a shared vision for equity and on circumstances within their control.
- **Disciplined action:** These adults understand concrete actions that hinder or advance efforts with equity.

How to Build a Working Definition of Equity

So how can leaders build a cohesive mentality around equity? Let's look at two foundational steps.

Step 1: Clarify the Term

As we learned from our urban school principal, don't assume that everyone understands the term. Although equity is often perceived as fairness for all, the term *fairness* can easily create challenges. Some may believe that fairness for all is about equality or about like conditions for everyone. According to Baruti Kafele (2021), "Over the years, countless students, particularly Black students, have suffered as the result of having been subjected to equality environments when an equitable learning experience was required" (p. 17). This first step in clarifying equity is about establishing an understanding with staff that equity is multifaceted and rooted in three principles. In an equitable environment,

1. Everyone is grounded in a common purpose.
2. Everyone gets what they need.
3. Everyone has open access to resources.

LEADERSHIP TIP

To develop a coherent equity statement and keep others on a path toward deeper understanding, persist in building that statement *together*. Defining equity for staff members will not work. You will establish coherence by collectively wrestling with understanding this term and coming to a group consensus. This is how ownership evolves. Remember, the key is to base your definition on the three equity principles: everyone is grounded in a common purpose, everyone gets what they need, and everyone has open access to resources.

Discussing these three principles gets everyone on the same page and acknowledges staff as key players in creating and living out a mission of equity. Here are the essential understandings:

- **Everyone is grounded in a common purpose.** To understand equity, we must first comprehend what everyone is entitled to and deserves. For example, all students deserve to be educated in a safe environment.
- **Everyone gets what they need.** Equity isn't about taking from the haves and giving to the have-nots; it's about recognizing what each and every student needs. An example of *equality* would be all students in a particular math class using the same textbook. However, *equity* requires educators to do more for some. Within that same math classroom, it would be equitable to consider resources beyond the textbook for students whose needs will not be met using only that.
- **Everyone has open access to resources.** Remember, equity opens doors rather than closes them. Giving students what they need should not lead to segregated practices. Take tracking and ability grouping, for example. Wanting students to learn with others at their level can certainly be a form of giving students what they need. However, it's also important to consider the downside—the social and emotional effect of this approach as well as the academic separation it creates. Finding balance will be crucial.

Figures 2.1 and 2.2 show two different activities leaders can use to help shape their staff's understanding of equity. Each activity is a precursor to building a working definition of the term with staff.

FIGURE 2.1

Clarifying Equity: Activity 1

Format: Staff meeting/workshop (45–60 minutes)

Materials: Chart paper, markers, and enough preprinted copies of the equity principles (see below) so that each staff member has an individual copy.

Activity:
1. Position posters around the room listing the *current state* and *future state* questions:

Current State
- What is our belief about equity?
- Does *fair* mean "equal for all"?
- What do our current approaches/actions indicate we believe?

Future State
If we were to exhibit the equity principles, what would equity...
- Look like?
- Sound like?
- Feel like?
  ...within our school environment?

2. In small groups, have staff brainstorm and record their thoughts concerning the current state questions.

3. After 10–15 minutes, give groups an opportunity to share their thinking aloud.

4. Turn the staff's attention to the three equity principles, reading them aloud.
- Everyone is grounded in a common purpose.
- Everyone gets what they need.
- Everyone has open access to resources.

5. Ask staff to consider the "Future State" questions in their small groups, brainstorming and recording their thoughts.

Conclusion: After the small groups have processed the future state questions (10–15 minutes), have staff share their thoughts with the whole group. Record common themes you're hearing. Have groups share any thoughts or themes that were not included in the share-out. Together, you will use this information to develop a working definition of equity.

FIGURE 2.2
Clarifying Equity: Activity 2

Format: Staff meeting/workshop (45–60 minutes)

Materials: Chart paper, markers, sticky notes, and enough preprinted copies of the equity principles (see below) so that each group has a copy.

Activity:

1. Start the conversation:

As part of the process of making sure each of our students succeeds, we're going to have continual conversations that dive deeper into equity. This will enable us to gain a common understanding and establish a new normal in how we address inequities.

2. Introduce the principles:

I've placed a sheet of paper on each of your tables that outlines the three principles of equity. We're going to use these principles to generate a consensus that will enable us to create a definition of equity that is unique to our environment and that represents our vision and mission for equity. But first, it's important to think about how our definition can and will be grounded in each principle of equity.

- *Everyone is grounded in a common purpose.*
- *Everyone gets what they need.*
- *Everyone has open access to resources.*

3. Ask the groups to review the equity principles and record their collective responses to the following questions for each of the principles:

   1. What does this principle mean to you? (What are your initial reactions?)
   2. How do you think this leads to equity?
   3. What are some examples of what this would look like in our environment?

4. After the small groups have processed the principles and questions (10–15 minutes), give staff an opportunity to share their thoughts, listen in on other discussions, or do a gallery walk to observe others' thinking. As they are sharing out or doing a gallery walk, capture and display key points regarding the various responses to Questions 1 and 2.

Conclusion: Drawing staff's attention to the key points, have each table come up with one statement or belief that embodies the key points. Collect these statements. As a group, modify the statements to make each one more cohesive. Have staff vote on the one they believe is the most compelling.

As you can see, the second activity, as shown in Figure 2.2, calls for consensus about what constitutes equity. A word of caution: Waiting for 100 percent of the staff to get on board is not the most productive or realistic strategy. Consider *consensus* to mean "the will of the group." Here's a scoring criterion I like to use when considering consensus building and buy-in:

4 = Consensus is firmly in place (80 percent or more of the group are in agreement)

3 = Consensus is moderately in place (60–79 percent of the group are in agreement)

2 = Consensus is in a beginning phase (30–59 percent of the group are in agreement)

1 = There is no consensus (less than 30 percent of the group are in agreement)

The more staff you have showing positive engagement, the greater their ability to influence outcomes.

LEADERSHIP TIP

This book will provide several tools and activities to help you shape a clear understanding of equity among your staff. Begin with the end in mind by applying some of the concepts set forth in *Understanding by Design* (Wiggins & McTighe, 1998). The following questions can assist you in the planning phase:

- What do adults need to know and be able to do at the end of the discussion or activity? That is, how do we want minds to shift?
- How will we know when we have reached our goal? What signs will tell us that we're heading in the right direction?
- What will we do if minds don't shift or adults are stuck in their learning? How will we revisit learning or help those who struggle with this issue move forward?

Step 2: Build a Working Definition of Equity

After setting a foundational understanding of the term *equity*, we're now at our second crucial step: collaborating with staff to establish a working definition that serves the environment. Remember, a working definition must drive a culture through three key ideas: *purpose, accountability,* and *action*. To shape a definition that builds coherence around each component, staff members need to consider three questions:

1. Why equity? (purpose)
2. What is our responsibility? (accountability)
3. What actions are needed? (action)

Figure 2.3 illustrates how these questions support each key idea in a working definition.

FIGURE 2.3
Building a Working Definition of Equity

Defining Question	Key Idea
Why equity?	**Purpose:** Those who are not negatively affected by inequity can easily misunderstand the magnitude of its effect on others. A working definition clearly communicates a desired state concerning the student and adult experience.
What is our responsibility?	**Accountability:** For staff to assume responsibility for carrying out a vision for equity, a working definition must clarify that everyone is accountable for the vision's pursuit.
What actions are needed?	**Action:** To fulfill a vision for equity, staff must understand what actions are required. A working definition will outline specific actions to take.

In this second step, staff need to understand why a working definition of equity is necessary within the environment. Start by having them look at available building data—data that speak to academics, behavior, and student satisfaction. They can use this information to build a definition that is informed by current conditions. The following questions are helpful in making sense of the data through a lens of equity (Chapter 5 provides an in-depth look at data use):

• Are some groups of students receiving access to advanced-level work or courses at higher rates than other groups?
• Are some groups of students being excluded from school at disproportionate rates?

- Are some groups of students being held to higher-level academic expectations or held to higher grading standards?
- Are some groups of students feeling disconnected from school?

Here's how a veteran principal guided her staff in building a working definition of equity after collectively reviewing the data. She had staff members assemble in small groups to respond to three questions about the core ideas of purpose, accountability, and action:

- **Why equity?** Based on your group's observation, why is equity needed?
- **What is our responsibility?** Thinking about the data and our conversations about the three core principles—everyone is grounded in a common purpose, everyone gets what they need, and everyone has open access to resources—what must we hold ourselves accountable for in honoring equity?
- **What actions are needed?** Based on your conversations, what steps must we commit to take?

Each group had approximately 25 minutes to respond to each question, and their responses, which they noted on a form, had to align with the data they had examined. Groups were asked to record no more than four thoughts or responses to each question and to prioritize which ideas were the most important. At the end of the discussion, the principal collected all the forms. She then compiled the staff's thinking by capturing the similarities in the responses. Here's what she recorded:

- **Purpose: Why equity?**
  - There's a disproportionality in our academic and behavior data.
  - Minority students are not adequately represented in gifted programs.
  - Minority students feel disconnected from school, according to climate survey data.
  - There's a disproportionality in referrals for special education among race groups.
- **Accountability: What is our responsibility?**
  - We need to take ownership of the educational experiences occurring in our school.

—We need to understand the cultural barriers and differences that exist in our environment.

—We need to monitor our progress and growth in terms of creating a more equitable environment.

—We need to prioritize teaching that speaks to the cultural needs of our students.

- **Action: What actions are needed?**

—We need to have difficult conversations in response to our data.

—We need to examine our practices and policies for inequities.

—We need to reflect on our personal biases to build self-awareness.

—We need to implement culturally responsive instruction.

The principal showed the staff their collective thinking before presenting her condensed version. Then they worked to create one belief statement to align with each question. Here are the statements that the staff came up with:

- **Why equity? (purpose):** All students have the right to reach their potential.
- **What is our responsibility? (accountability):** As a building, we must honor differences and meet individual needs.
- **What actions are needed? (action):** Equity and data must be part of everything we do.

The final step was using the statements to create this working definition of equity that was centered around students:

All students have the right to meet their full potential. This means that we will be intentional in creating systems that honor and bring awareness to educational differences and unique needs. As a result, we commit to explicitly embedding and monitoring equity in our culture through our conversations, practices, and policies.

The process of constructing the working definition enabled staff to decide on a common goal for equity and agree on actionable steps. Compare this working definition with the equity statement introduced earlier: "We are dedicated to ensuring an equitable learning environment for every student, family, and staff member regardless of background."

What do you notice about the two statements? Which essential ideas are missing from the original statement?

LEADERSHIP TIP

An equity vision statement that's not coupled with action is useless. Use the formulated statement to generate meaningful acts and to hold the environment accountable to its purpose. Plan actions that align with the words written in your statement, and hold the vision up against undesirable actions that others are taking. It's easy to fall into the trap of writing a well-thought-out vision statement and just assume it will lead to positive change. Commit to the process by using your equity statement to monitor daily activities. To assist you in this work, the coming chapters will offer ideas of how to support your vision through a monitoring process.

Making the Most of Time

Creating a working definition of equity is about bringing clarity and focus—coherence—to the process of pursuing equity. Captured equity statements should be embedded in the culture through conversation and serve as a litmus test for current and future policies, practices, and actions.

It's up to leaders to create space for the work of achieving coherence. That might mean setting a standing time for a brief check-in at each faculty meeting, during which staff identify and reflect on actions that support or are in opposition of an equity definition. It could be done through "sticky note voting" on chart paper (which allows the leader to collect and assess themes for future conversations) or as a whole-group share-out. The critical role of the leader in these circumstances is to reinforce the vision of the working definition of equity and ensure staff continue to act intentionally to bring that written definition to life within the environment. Remember, when staff members come together around a purpose, it results in increased engagement, fosters accountability and trust, improves decision making, and cultivates a stronger adult bond.

Next Steps for Leaders: Clarify the Work

We can't create what we fail to understand. Strategic leadership is required to build a level of coherence that results in equity. Leverage data to establish a definition of equity that communicates purpose, calls for accountability, and expects action. Bringing a definition of equity to life is imperative. When a definition is truly working, it guides adults through purposeful movements and actions. The formula is simple: *Clarity = Change.*

Ask yourself...

- To what extent do I sense a clear understanding of equity within my environment?
- To what degree is our current definition of equity working? How is it student-centered? How is it creating action?

3

Creating Discomfort

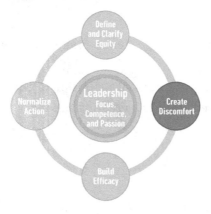

"A great many people think they are thinking when all
they are doing is rearranging their prejudices."

—William James

We can change policy, provide a multicultural curriculum, and even mandate culturally relevant practices, but no top-down effort will matter much if staff are unable to face and navigate through learned beliefs. The true work of equity is necessarily invasive because it must reconstruct the heart.

The second component of the Equity Leadership Framework is creating a culture of discomfort. This means establishing an environment in which avoidance has no place and adults feel safe to challenge racial inequities, deficit ideologies, and the status quo. Race *does* matter, and adequately addressing equity can only take place through a willingness to get *constructively uncomfortable* by having intentional dialogue that is conscious of race.

Race, as a topic, remains the most overlooked, feared, and unnamed factor that impedes equity in many of our schools. In her book *Colormute*, Mica Pollock (2004) shared the following conversation she had with a teacher named John. It highlights how easily the topic of race is avoided in schools:

> **Me:** Do you think any kids are falling through the cracks this year?
> **John:** Oh yeah, kids wandering around the halls, mostly African-American males and females.
> **Me:** Do people talk about the fact that it's mostly African-Americans wandering around the halls?
> **John:** No, it hasn't been brought up yet [*with a laugh in his voice*]. But it will very soon!
> **Me:** Why, do you think?
> **John:** It needs to be talked about.
> **Me:** So you think it will be?
> **John:** Overall under the headline of "attendance and cutting." I'll bring it up if no one else does. (p. 179)

Notice that although John has an innate understanding that race is a concern, he's reluctant to label and confront the problem. His choice to address the issue of "attendance and cutting" invites us to ask what is preventing him from calling attention to the fact that Black students are missing class? Better yet, what unwritten rules within the culture promote avoidance of this issue?

Creating a culture of constructive discomfort means confronting stereotypes, misperceptions, and systemic conditions that negatively affect underserved students. Yes, this *is* likely to be uncomfortable, but it's absolutely necessary. You can't design an effective solution unless you have an accurate understanding of the problem you're facing.

Microaggressions

Educators can inadvertently prevent students from benefiting from learning opportunities, acting as gatekeepers who determine who will and will not experience academic success (Peterson, 1999). Generally, they assume this role unknowingly, suggesting that many circumstances that undesirably affect students of color have nothing to do with ill intent or malice. But the impact of their gatekeeping is nonetheless real. Here's an illustration.

Jaylon, a Black 6th grader, is a promising young scholar with a gift in math and science. He was identified for the gifted and talented program in the 4th grade, specifically for his talent in math. During the spring of Jaylon's 6th grade year, his norm-referenced winter assessment math scores indicated his ability was equivalent to that of an 11th grader. Success in his school's High Ability Learner program, along with a scale score 11 points above the prerequisite for the advanced algebra course, meant Jaylon was on track to receive the highest recommendation for elementary students moving into 7th grade math. However, when it came time for Jaylon's general education classroom teacher to fill out the recommendation form for middle school classes, she did *not* recommend him for the advanced or top-tier math class. Here is the emailed message she sent to Jaylon's parents:

> Hi! We are now being asked to place the students in their middle school math program. I have decided—based on the prerequisite numbers given to me by the middle school for adequate progress results, as well as classroom assessment grades and other factors—to place your student in the *middle math class*, which is 7th grade Pre-Algebra Advanced. *A side note:* Most kids in my class will be placed in Intro to Pre-Algebra. Only one to two students qualify for Algebra Advanced course, which is an 8th grade class.
>
> Thanks! Please let me know if you have any questions or concerns.

Jaylon certainly had his moments of being silly in class, but his parents were confused by this placement decision. Hadn't he earned all *As* in math on his report card? Taking the teacher up on her offer, they emailed to ask if it were possible to get Jaylon into the advanced class. Here is the response they received:

> The middle school math teachers said that Algebra Advanced was two to four hours of homework each night and that students shouldn't take that course unless they are going for a math degree. I will put Jaylon in the advanced course if you want; it's your call. I wasn't sure that he wanted to "live" for math. I figured he'd be doing sports, church, etc. Again, I will do what you want. Let me know.

Jaylon's teacher is well respected by students and highly recommended by families each year. However, within an environment where race and racial inequities are rarely acknowledged and more rarely discussed, teachers like Jaylon's will likely remain unaware of their role in contributing to racial stereotypes and inequalities. Placement in the more advanced course would have provided Jaylon with appropriate academic challenge and would have also broken the familiar pattern of Black male students being absent from rigorous courses. Recommending Jaylon for a math class beneath his cognitive level would put him on an educational track that might limit his future opportunities and perpetuate the achievement gap.

Such actions are a form of *microaggression*. The term was coined more than 50 years ago to explain unintentional and relatively small offenses that reinforce derogatory stereotypes (Pierce, 1970). Microaggressions are often unknowingly committed by well-meaning individuals. For example, Jaylon's teacher acknowledged he had academic potential by supporting his participation in the gifted program during his 6th grade year. However, her rationale for not recommending Jaylon for the advanced course—that he probably wouldn't want to "live for math," that sports and church activities would most likely take up a good bit of his time—fits a stereotypical narrative about young Black men. Such microaggressions create prolonged effects on students who experience them consistently within the learning environment. A considerable body of research indicates their pervasiveness and harmful effects (Boysen, 2012; Suárez-Orozco et al., 2015; Sue, 2010). Cultures of constructive discomfort are the only way to eradicate misguided thoughts and perceptions that easily interfere with the schooling of students of color.

Here's another example of a microaggression observed by a principal in a 10th grade history class. Students were working in groups preparing for a debate; the teacher was walking around the room monitoring each discussion. She overheard a Black student say to his group, "I'm just gonna keep it 100: I don't understand why this is something we have to conversate about." The teacher walked over to the group and told the student, "You mean *converse* about." The teacher then gave the following guidance to the entire group: "In a debate, be sure to use proper English and avoid using slang. This will help you get your point across by ensuring that others can follow and understand."

Although this teacher may have assumed that this feedback was setting up this student for success, the hidden message delivered was that the student did not speak proper English and that it wasn't acceptable for him to be his authentic self. The phrasing also communicated an assumption about *whose* ability to follow and understand should be a priority (others who use "proper English"). Students of color who are inundated with these subtle suggestions are susceptible to mental angst and emotional trauma. Such incidents can enhance the identity struggles and inferiority that students of color are naturally inclined to experience while navigating an environment that enforces a dominant cultural narrative. Harm may not have been intended, but harm is real. Figure 3.1 offers some additional classroom examples of microaggressions influenced by race.

FIGURE 3.1

Examples of Microaggressions in the Classroom

- Arranging classroom seating in a way that singles out students based on racial background, such as having all Black students sit together in the back of the room or near the teacher.
- Asking a question that requires students of color to speak for their entire race.
- Celebrating in an over-the-top way or publicly admiring common things that students of color do, such as dressing in a certain way, speaking grammatically, or answering a question correctly.
- Anticipating the responses of students of color or questioning the credibility and validity of stories they have shared.
- Continually asking students of color lower-level academic questions.
- Calling out the behaviors of students of color more than those of others in the class who are acting similarly.
- Pointing out to students of color that they aren't "applying themselves."
- Telling students of color not to worry about completing certain math problems because those questions are "too difficult."
- Quickly calling on a neighbor to help a student of color who does not respond to a question correctly.
- Continuing to mispronounce the name of students of color after they have repeatedly provided correction.
- Heavily enforcing rules for students of color as opposed to doing so with other students.
- Labeling or calling out the actions of students of color as "aggressive."

In a survey conducted by Weinstein (2002) that examined urban 4th graders' perceptions on their own intelligence, nearly two-thirds of the respondents identified their teachers' remarks or actions as the basis for how intelligent they believed themselves to be; only 5 percent of the students alluded to peers or parents as influencing their view of their intelligence. This study drives home just how important it is for school leaders to build cultures of constructive discomfort that challenge educators to be deeply aware of how what they do and say can unknowingly prolong inequity. Being *comfortably uncomfortable* is a shift in thinking; it's how we disrupt unwarranted practices and create systemic change. To achieve this, educators need space to reflect on and discuss race, both privately and publicly.

Roadblocks to Getting Uncomfortable

There are two hurdles to creating an environment that embraces constructive discomfort.

Fear of the "Racist" Label

The fear of being called or labeled a racist can manifest in a couple of ways.

A commitment to colorblindness. Here, individuals assert that race "will not be seen" within the educational environment. Although one might view this as fighting for equality, that's a misinterpretation. Theoretically, not taking account of one's skin color should help establish a culture in which discrimination is a nonfactor and all individuals develop a strong sense of acceptance. However, this view fails to accept the daily life and school experiences of those who know that color *does* matter, because their social interaction with the world clearly proves it does. A lens of colorblindness simply does not help the cause of individuals of color (Tarca, 2005) or advance equity. Colorblindness enables separation.

Inhibited awareness. Because individuals don't want to be thought of or viewed as racist, this perpetuates environments where adults never adequately address errored thinking. They tend to suppress questions that might help them navigate their thinking around race so that they will not offend anyone. This inability to talk through one's wonderings invites a continuation of thought processes that unknowingly exacerbate and prolong inequity.

A Limited Understanding of Privilege

The second hurdle to an environment of constructive discomfort is an inaccurate understanding of the concept of privilege.

Too often, approaches to privilege focus solely on *white privilege*. This not only opens the doors to a response of self-defense or denial but also ignores a far-reaching reality about privilege—that it stretches beyond the confines of a particular race group. Privilege is, in fact, circumstantial. Thus, all educators should explore their circumstances to detect how or if privilege is swaying their views, conditions, and interactions. Consider this: even teachers who share the same skin tone and were raised in similar environments as their underserved students are set apart from these students by virtue of both age and education (Scott, 2017).

Let's look for a moment at unearned privilege or, for the purposes of this discussion, *positional freedom*. Positional freedom implies that certain factors that are naturally bestowed upon us place us in a position of advantage by granting us freedoms that others don't have access to. For example, consider the experience of going to the dealership to buy a new car as a man as opposed to a woman, being able-bodied as opposed to living with physical challenges, or being considered economically well off as opposed to being seen as poor. Each consideration can place individuals at an advantage over others who don't have the same liberty to create similar conditions or circumstances.

Race is another factor that naturally creates conditions of positional freedom. For example, when adults share a culture with the students they teach, students within that culture have access to a social bond that is not instinctively available to students who don't share that culture. Students who share their teacher's culture have positional freedom; they can be who they authentically are without fear of judgment. Moreover, the teacher can speak to these students without fear of racial implications.

The historical disadvantages that students of color have long endured in schools also allude to positional freedoms. White students traditionally receive greater access to advanced courses and to a culturally relevant curriculum; they are typically held to higher expectations, and they often learn with a teacher whose culture and values mirror their own. They are exposed to more career choices and, therefore, will benefit from a higher future earning potential. Leaders must promote mindfulness around the fact that all circumstances are not created equal and that some individuals are better positioned than others to access additional freedoms.

Cultures that refuse to explore the concept of privilege persist as institutions where adults are less likely to recognize and disassemble systemic conditions that preserve privilege. Denying the notion of privilege can only result in a misunderstanding of any advantages some might have over others. This invites a misdiagnosis of the circumstances faced by those on the opposite end of our positional freedom and an inability to distinguish who is marginalized. Being unaware of our advantaged position also decreases our ability to empathize with, and thus adequately support, the disadvantaged.

School leaders can't afford to accept an unawareness of positional freedom on the part of those they're counting on to establish equity. If your faculty and staff are unaware of their privilege or dismissive of the concept, they will likely see your push for constructive discomfort as unnecessary or even destructive.

LEADERSHIP TIP

Even among a staff that is positive about equity work, conversations about privilege can elicit pushback and denial. Here, I think it's worth remembering that, as philosopher John Rawls (1971) argued, we can more objectively assess how a just society should operate and see how privilege can irresponsibly put some at a disadvantage when we take our own personal circumstances out of the equation. Who we are can keep us from seeing the full picture of the world around us. Helping individuals approach the topic of race with the understanding that they have blind spots can help them realize their positional freedom and better serve those with greater or more acute needs.

Of course, some may perceive this conversation as a form of personal attack. If you have staff members who feel stigmatized by being recognized as privileged, stress that receiving positional freedom influenced by race does not imply any of the following:

- That you haven't worked hard or earned what you have received in life.
- That you haven't faced trials or setbacks in your life.
- That your race at some point hasn't worked against you.
- That this is something you have asked for.
- That you are voluntarily cheating the system.
- That you intentionally embrace dominance over others.
- Anything about your personal character.

Creating a Comfortably Uncomfortable Culture

As Radd and colleagues (2021) have pointed out, "Some educators feel that their experiences and education have fully prepared them to work effectively with students from all backgrounds and that they have nothing left to learn about educational equity and how best to serve their students" (p. 23). This false assumption affirms the need for a wake-up call of constructive discomfort. Historically, schools have revealed they are not fundamentally constructed to educate students of color; the disproportionality in learning signifies a lack of awareness, expertise, and capacity to affirm the needs of oppressed students (Singleton & Linton, 2005). Leaders must support a culture that gets comfortable with being uncomfortable because such an environment is crucial to narrowing educational opportunity gaps for students of color.

Getting uncomfortable is more than just orchestrating opportunities for adults to think critically about race. Nor does requiring individuals to be physically present for these conversations prevent some from opting out mentally. Leaders must help staff build both the skill and will to become vulnerable enough to purposefully engage, and they need to do this without placing blame. Getting mired in feelings of racial guilt or shame is not fruitful for these conversations.

The objective for leaders is to unite staff in understanding the root causes of existing inequitable practices, thoughts, and actions. Leaders can build this awareness by leveraging a continual process involving three *C*s: contemplation, conversation, and consciousness. It's about helping individuals get outside what Ross (2013) called *cultural bubbles*. Our cultural bubbles are too often reinforced by a belief that "likeness" is a strength; thus, it's imperative that educators learn to see beyond themselves. To combat this desire to gravitate toward likeness, leaders must provide staff with continual opportunities for contemplation and conversation so they can delve into morals and values, and into experiences with race and biases, to promote effective levels of consciousness. Without such spaces, adults within schools will lack the wherewithal to consistently address conditions that allow students of color to experience inequality.

In her book *Why Are All the Black Kids Sitting Together in the Cafeteria?* (1997), Beverly Tatum writes,

I have heard many people say, "But I don't know enough… I don't have enough of the facts to be able to speak up about racism or anything else!" They are not alone. We have all been miseducated in this regard. Educating ourselves and others is an essential step in the process for change. Few of us have been taught to think critically about issues of social injustice. We have been taught not to notice or to accept our present situation as a given, "the way it is." (p. 203)

Implementing the three Cs not only enhances awareness but also incites the mindfulness that promotes purposeful actions. But before exploring each of the Cs in depth, let's consider an essential idea that paves the way for sustainability of practice. I call this *win the preliminaries*. It's about doing the necessary groundwork to ensure that the buildingwide practices of contemplation, conversation, and consciousness can succeed.

Win the Preliminaries

For leaders, attempts to dive deep into the topic of race often fail at takeoff because of the natural friction that occurs between wanting to engage staff in difficult conversations and waiting for the right moment. There's understandably some hesitation in placing the culture of a building at risk by intensifying dialogue around race. Thus, the topic of race commonly gets placed on the back burner because it's much easier for organizations to rationalize that "the time is just not right."

Winning the preliminaries is not about determining whether we should talk; rather, it's about becoming aware of the structures in place to ensure we move competently as we do talk. Leaders need a clear understanding of the collaborative supports and cooperative mindsets that are already in place in the building to better grasp the degree to which constructive conversations are possible and where missteps might occur. In other words, to win the preliminaries, leaders must find the balance between moving conversations too quickly and not engaging at all.

Using Climate Assessment Tools

To determine the status of a building's collaborative supports and cooperative mindsets, climate assessment tools and activities (as shown in Figures 3.2 through 3.5) can help.

FIGURE 3.2

Leadership Climate Assessment and Evidence Collection: Activity 1

Format: Leadership team meeting (30–45 minutes)

Materials: Leadership Climate Assessment (Figure 3.4; download at www.ascd .org/EquityLeadershipHandouts); Evidence Collection Form for a Leadership Climate Assessment (Appendix Tool A; download at www.ascd.org/EquityLeadershipToolset); chart paper; and writing materials

Activity:

1. Have each member of the leadership team fill out the **Leadership Climate Assessment** and the **Evidence Collection Form for a Leadership Climate Assessment** to determine the degree to which current conditions would support the staff's ability to successfully navigate the challenges of equity work.

2. As participants read each statement on the Leadership Climate Assessment, have them use the rating scale included in the assessment (it's also shown below) to score each statement. As participants rank the statements, have them consider the following question: *What specific evidence strongly supports my thinking?* Ask them to document that evidence on the Evidence Collection Form.

   Rating Scale
   4 = Firmly in Place (80 percent or more)
   3 = Moderately in Place (60–79 percent)
   2 = Beginning Phase (30–59 percent)
   1 = Nonexistent (Less than 30 percent/no measures in place to support this statement)

3. Once members score each element, have them tally their point totals for group discussion:

   Supportive Environment = 52–64 total points
   Relatively Supportive Environment = 39–51 total points
   Need More Support = 16–38 total points

4. As a team, go through each statement on the Leadership Climate Assessment, sharing individual ratings and evidence from the Evidence Collection Form.

5. As you discuss each statement, weigh each member's evidence and ratings to look for consensus within the group. Use a blank Leadership Climate Assessment form to capture the group's consensus ranking for each statement.

6. Tally the points and overall score to determine the current status.

   Supportive Environment = 52–64 total points
   Relatively Supportive Environment = 39–51 total points
   Need More Support = 16–38 total points

Closing: Continue to the Staff Climate Assessment: Activity 2 (see Figure 3.3).

FIGURE 3.3
Staff Climate Assessment: Activity 2

Format: Leadership team meeting (30–45 minutes)

Materials: Staff Climate Assessment (Figure 3.5; download at www.ascd.org/EquityLeadershipHandouts); chart paper; and writing materials

Note: The Staff Climate Assessment correlates with the Leadership Climate Assessment (see Figure 3.4). Leaders can use that form to gain additional information about current building conditions.

Activity:

1. Before the meeting, have staff members individually complete the **Staff Climate Assessment,** which focuses on conditions necessary for staff to engage effectively in equity work, and tally their scores. Have the leadership team chart staff scores (using tally marks) as follows:

   Rating Scale
   Firmly in Place = 69–80 total points
   Moderately in Place = 49–68 total points
   Beginning Phase = 20–48 total points
   Nonexistent = Less than 20 points

2. After tallying results of the entire staff, discuss the following questions:
   • How do the staff's perceptions align with the **Leadership Climate Assessment**?
   • How do the staff's perceptions differ?
   • How supportive is the environment in terms of handling difficult conversations?

Closing:
Summarize the outcome of the activity. If leadership and staff believe the needed conditions are firmly in place, move forward with planning equity conversations centered around race. If discrepancies exist, identify problems and develop any plans or steps needed to support future conversations. Determine if you will need to repeat this activity at another date or time for monitoring.

FIGURE 3.4
Leadership Climate Assessment

Climate Components	4 = Firmly in Place 3 = Moderately in Place 2 = Beginning Phase 1 = Nonexistent
Collaborative Practice	
Structured opportunities are in place for staff to problem solve.	4 3 2 1
Staff receive consistent and timely feedback.	4 3 2 1
Staff are effectively using established time together to discuss self- and school improvement.	4 3 2 1
Peer learning opportunities are provided and sought after.	4 3 2 1
Mindset	
Change is met with a sense of optimism (adults are willing to try new things and use positive framing).	4 3 2 1
Staff conversations focus on areas within their control.	4 3 2 1
Staff hold themselves accountable when students fail.	4 3 2 1
Staff hold one another accountable to current policies and practices.	4 3 2 1
Reflective Practice	
Opportunities exist for professional development through continual self-reflection and monitoring of personal growth.	4 3 2 1
Staff take advantage of opportunities to reflect on their practice.	4 3 2 1
Staff routinely use data-based decision making.	4 3 2 1
Staff seek to understand how their actions affect student learning.	4 3 2 1
Culture	
Staff acknowledge cultural experiences and backgrounds in classrooms.	4 3 2 1
Staff consistently focus on meeting the social-emotional needs of challenging students.	4 3 2 1
Punitive practices are not endorsed in classrooms.	4 3 2 1
Professional development is designed with diverse student groups in mind.	4 3 2 1
Point Totals	

Collaborative Practice:		Mindset:		Reflective Practice:		Culture:		OVERALL TOTAL:	

FIGURE 3.5
Staff Climate Assessment

Climate Components	4 = Always 3 = Almost Always 2 = Occasionally 1 = Never
Collaborative Practice	
I have opportunities to formally collaborate with peers and colleagues.	4 3 2 1
I routinely receive formal and informal feedback.	4 3 2 1
I value and implement the feedback I receive.	4 3 2 1
I frequently converse with peers to learn how I can improve the school and learning environment.	4 3 2 1
Mindset	
I believe my efforts make a difference in the learning environment.	4 3 2 1
I believe my colleagues think their efforts make a difference and act accordingly.	4 3 2 1
I focus on areas within my control.	4 3 2 1
I believe I am responsible for student learning and for contributing to a positive school culture.	4 3 2 1
Reflective Practice	
I am encouraged to self-reflect, and I receive opportunities to do so as part of my professional development.	4 3 2 1
I regularly self-reflect on my practice.	4 3 2 1
I use data in my decision-making process.	4 3 2 1
I seek to understand the effect of my actions.	4 3 2 1
Culture	
I acknowledge the cultural experiences and backgrounds of others.	4 3 2 1
I am sensitive to the social-emotional challenges students face.	4 3 2 1
I believe the use of stronger reprimands improves student behavior.	4 3 2 1
My peers and colleagues use punitive practices to manage behavior.	4 3 2 1

Point Totals								
Collaborative Practice:		**Mindset:**		**Reflective Practice:**		**Culture:**		**OVERALL TOTAL:**

These tools enable users to discover clear indicators for each element listed—for example, whether staff hold themselves accountable when students fail or endorse punitive practices in response to student misbehavior—and they promote rich conversations as a result. The more indicators that are firmly in place, the greater the probability that adults within a culture will work through a nuanced conversation.

LEADERSHIP TIP

Here is some guidance about how to use the assessment tools:

- **Know the intent.** Leverage each tool to win the preliminaries by identifying gaps in leadership support and determining the right level of entry based on areas of perceived weakness. The climate assessment tools should lead to deeper talks regarding factors that influence current conditions and where teams should place their efforts when providing support.
- **There are no absolutes.** The assessment tools are not about absolutes. Nevertheless, they can provide insight about how to sensibly proceed. For example, if scores fall between 3 and 4 on the assessments, meaning that a number of supports are already in place, then a team should consider moving on to tackle other issues while continuing to maintain or strengthen collaborative and reflective practices. If results fall primarily in the 1 to 2 range, which means that many of those supports might be lacking, it might be beneficial to spend additional time putting the right structures in place to support more in-depth conversations. Falling in this lower range does not mean that all efforts to address race must wait or stop; levels of conversation or activities can occur if you conduct them in an effective way.

A Look at the Three Cs

Now that we understand the importance of evaluating a culture of readiness, let's get back to building a cohesive awareness around race using the three Cs: contemplation, conversation, and consciousness.

Contemplation

Dismantling inequitable conditions experienced by students of color involves leadership actions that grow the level of consciousness within the culture. Consciousness does not happen without contemplation. And what do we get out of contemplation? It's vital to self-evolution and a prerequisite for becoming attentive to implicit biases and conditions that we cannot see. Creating adequate time and space for staff to deeply explore their thinking is a moral imperative for leaders.

Neglecting to allow staff to spend time exploring issues rooted in race can pose a substantial threat to systemic change efforts. The fact is, we all fall victim to autopilot moments, thinking and acting without full awareness of importance or consequence. This becomes a dangerous proposition when considering the more than one thousand decisions that teachers make each day, decisions that are frequently driven by a monocultural lens. To remove barriers that impede the learning of students of color, teachers must be able to acknowledge their thinking. Providing continual opportunities to pause and contemplate increases teachers' capacity to be aware in the moment. Also, consistently examining race can build a level of automaticity and resiliency when it comes to pushing past perceptual limitations to identify and respond to inequity.

An inescapable reality when setting aside time for staff to think critically about race is that everyone will not have the same level of enthusiasm or commitment or receive the same benefits from the process. Don't let this derail efforts to afford adults the necessary space and time to practice a habit of reflection. Remember, too, that the value of this process isn't determined by how quickly or slowly staff catch on. Throughout the process, subtle changes will occur in their thought processes and actions. We can trust that if people are immersed in the right environment long enough, they will experience some positive effects, even if only on a small scale.

Part of producing the right level of exposure as a leader involves consistently inviting staff to explore race using a variety of perspectives:

- In the context of themselves (*What is my individual relationship with race?*);
- In the context of their relationships with others (*What are my experiences in relation to what others encounter?*); and
- In the context of systemic challenges within the school or larger system (*What are the institutional conditions that marginalize specific groups?*).

Each viewpoint presents an opportunity not only to affect the core of what someone believes but also to allow for an enhanced level of empathy and action.

For example, leaders might dedicate a portion of each staff meeting to a process of reflection. They could invite staff to ponder a question while taking a moment to journal their thoughts. Although not everyone finds comfort in journaling, having staff record their thinking is a way for them to self-monitor their thought patterns over time. By doing so, they may well start detecting unfavorable ideologies or conditions that oppress students of color.

Figure 3.6 shows a contemplation play card that leaders can use to provide focused opportunities for contemplation. Remember, the objective is to get staff to think critically on a consistent enough basis for creating change. Here are three steps to using the play card:

1. **Establish the purpose for contemplation.** With the three viewpoints in mind (personal, interpersonal, and global), determine how you want staff to think critically about race. Knowing the purpose enables you to be more intentional in planning a reflective question with a specific influence on areas of needed growth.
2. **Determine the areas of focus.** Discuss with staff your rationale for selecting a given area of focus (e.g., life experiences, classroom conditions, building conditions). Addressing a diversity of focus areas will enable staff to recognize that race shows up in a multitude of settings.
3. **Design a reflective question to push critical thinking.** Now it's time to think about how you will push staff's thinking. Here you will craft a reflective question that facilitates contemplation around critical aspects pertaining to race.

As Figure 3.6 shows, you can tweak any of the prompts to fit a given intention for reflection.

Let's look at an actual example of how you might use the contemplation play card and how it can lead to positive results. The following is a conversation I had with a teacher who was reflecting on the question *How is my cultural narrative affecting my interaction with families?* Notice how having time to contemplate and self-monitor her thinking led to a deeper understanding about her beliefs:

FIGURE 3.6
Contemplation Play Card

What is the purpose of contemplation?

- **Personal:** To explore individual experiences with race
- **Interpersonal:** To consider personal experiences with race in relation to what others encounter
- **Global:** To examine how the larger system (school or district) marginalizes specific groups

What is the area of focus?

Life Experiences	Building Conditions
• Educational • Family • Societal • Positional freedom	• Policy practices (e.g., grading) • Procedures • Programs (e.g., special education, gifted) • Student recognition • Behavior

Classroom Conditions	Data
• Relationships with families/students • Written rules/expectations • Classroom management/behavior practices • Instructional practices	• Formal and informal classroom data • Perceptual (e.g., climate survey) data • Classroom/program enrollment data • Suspension/student dropout data • Standardized testing data

Critical Thinking Prompts

- How is my thinking relating to _____ (e.g., discipline) reflective of my upbringing or family viewpoints?
- How am I/are we culturally responsive in my/our _____ (e.g., grading practices)?
- In looking at _____ (e.g., the academic gaps in my classroom), how might my/our thoughts or actions perpetuate bias or known stereotypes?
- When implementing _____ (e.g., buildingwide behavior expectations), do we do it broadly or do we consider the cultural differences of various students? Explain.
- What are the possible implications of positional freedom when it comes to _____ (e.g., suspensions)?
- When it comes to _____ (e.g., families), do any of my/our assumptions hint at racial bias? Explain.
- How is my cultural narrative or positional freedom influencing my _____ (e.g., communication with families)?
- What does my/our _____ (e.g., program enrollment) say about student access or the experience of others?
- What might be the positive or negative reaction of someone who thinks, feels, or looks differently?
- What would this _____ (e.g., policy) look like from an unbiased point of view?
- Looking at my/our _____ (e.g., climate survey), do any common narratives point to conditions of racial segregation?
- Assuming race influences my/our _____ (e.g., interactions with students), how might it show up?

(continued)

FIGURE 3.6—(continued)
Contemplation Play Card
Critical Thinking Prompts—(continued)
• Does my/our _____ (e.g., recognition of students) place students equally at an advantage? Explain. • How might my cultural lens be affecting my ability to relate? What am I struggling to see? • Would I feel differently if this situation/circumstance were happening to me or to someone I cared about? Explain. • Does my/our _____ (e.g., buildingwide practices) extend beyond a monocultural lens? Explain. • Is what we see _____ (e.g., in our data) a one-time occurrence, or is something more systemic happening? Explain. • Based on _____ (e.g., our special education population), does our current culture inadvertently harbor conditions of racial segregation? • Are my/our actions, feelings, or results free from unfavorable conditions of race? Explain.

Ms. Parker: When reflecting on this question, I immediately wrote about a Black student in my class whose family I had a strained relationship with. I didn't have any major concerns with the student, but his father always seemed to be questioning my grading and classroom practices. The dad was a larger Black man with a deep voice who quite frankly intimidated and flustered me with questions about his son's learning—questions I felt were unreasonable expectations for his son.

Me: What do you feel you aren't able to see?

Ms. Parker: This part of the question really bothered me. I really wanted to believe there wasn't anything I couldn't see, but I pushed myself to search for something.

Me: Pushed yourself how?

Ms. Parker: I asked myself a difficult question: *How might I be part of the problem?* I thought about the time I asked the principal to sit in on a meeting with this dad because I wasn't comfortable sitting with him alone. It dawned on me that it was the only family conference where I requested the principal be present.

Me: Why is that a problem?

Ms. Parker: I'm embarrassed to say, but I realized that I didn't make this same request for other families who were just as forthright about their kids. There were white parents of students in my class who were even more persistent than this dad was, but I did not ask that my principal be present at any of their conferences.

As this example illustrates, contemplation can play a considerable role in establishing change within an individual. This teacher clearly is beginning to take advantage of the reflection process at a level that will enable her to continue to grow. Of course, not everyone will come to a significant revelation effortlessly or in a short span of time. Consider how you might leverage staff meetings, teacher collaborative time, or coaching and evaluation to enable teachers to reflect. This will be important to build and support the capacity to effectively engage in our next *C*—conversation.

Conversation

Let's begin by revisiting Terry, the middle school principal whose efforts we looked at in Chapter 1. You may recall that he was responding to trend data indicating a disproportionality in suspensions and academic achievement regarding students of color. One approach that led to some success was focusing on areas within staff control—in this case, on culturally responsive and restorative practices. The school did witness a decline in student discipline incidences and an increase in academics, but neither result spoke to the disparity existing among racial groups. Although the teachers on Terry's staff had a clearer focus, they needed a safe space to engage in critical conversations about race.

It's the leader's role to establish safe conditions that will enable others to willfully get comfortably uncomfortable. The following three steps can set the foundation:

Step 1: Collectively establish conversation ground rules. Although we would like to believe that all adults will behave appropriately, talks centered on race can test character. Ground rules not only provide a sense of order, but also keep conversations on course. Having been a part of many racially charged conversations over the years, I recognize that it's easy for adults to lean into common patterns of behavior that keep dialogues stagnant. Here are some conversation pitfalls to watch out for:

- **Assuming one's view is widely accepted.** The presumption that our view is common or *normal* inadvertently places us in a position of dominance in the conversation.
- **Seeking to be "right" or "win" the conversation.** Approaching a conversation like a debate implies that we're not talking as part of a quest for learning but to win over our point. Seeking to be heard, not necessarily to be understood, takes the conversation nowhere.
- **Trying to justify or discredit someone's negative experience.** It's a mistake to try to convince someone that their experience is not real. If it's real to them, it has shaped who they are, and that's the person you're trying to get to know better.
- **Formulating opinions or judgments.** Forming judgments during conversation blocks us from hearing and diminishes understanding.
- **Speaking carelessly.** Never forget that words and tone matter. Each of us is certainly free to speak our personal truth, but we must also pay attention to how we share that truth. We may be able to rebound from mishaps with our words, but that becomes more challenging if our tone is abrasive.
- **Speaking for an entire racial group.** None of us can speak for an entire race, and no one should be inclined or feel compelled to do so.

A challenge in leading others to confront race through intentional conversations is getting them to a place of both give and take. To foster ownership and follow-through, collectively work with staff to determine the rules for engagement. Figure 3.7 presents an activity you might use to do this. The ABCs of Conversations About Race, as shown in Figure 3.8, is an integral part of the activity.

Step 2: Keep established rules front and center. As a group, staff may need to modify the rules of engagement as everyone adjusts to becoming comfortably uncomfortable. Different behaviors may emerge that current rules might not address. The act of talking through the rules provides added value and helps ensure an appropriate tone for the conversation. Be sure to keep the rules at the forefront; this emphasizes their importance and encourages participants to lean on them during crucial moments in the conversation.

FIGURE 3.7
Setting Conversation Conditions: Activity 1

Format: All-Staff Meeting (20–25 minutes)

Materials: Copies of The ABCs of Conversations About Race (Figure 3.8; download at www.ascd.org/EquityLeadershipHandouts) and two sets of different-colored markers or dot stickers (e.g., blue markers/stickers and yellow markers/stickers)

Activity:
1. Distribute copies of **The ABCs of Conversations About Race.** Ask staff to read the handout and reflect on how each element contributes to productive conversations or open dialogue.

2. Ask staff to identify on their individual copy of the handout (using one of the colored markers or dots) three to four elements that they would most like to see others exhibit during a conversation in order for them to feel valued and heard.

3. Ask staff to use the other marker/sticker (in a different color) to identify on their copy of the handout three to four elements they believe are most crucial for them to self-monitor for and exhibit during a conversation in order to ensure *others* feel valued and heard.

4. Ask each staff member to share, in pairs or their small groups, the elements they've selected. *Be sure to have them briefly discuss why they selected each.*

5. Once the share-out is complete (10–15 minutes), ask staff to make any modifications they would like to their selection. Explain that in future conversations, they will be asked to keep a copy of their conversational conditions in visible sight during discussions for accountability purposes.

Leadership teaching point: Before beginning discussions on race, provide space for staff to quickly review the desired norms. Be mindful of group size to keep conversations productive (3–5 people is optimal). An alternative strategy is to have staff come with a blank copy of **The ABCs of Conversations About Race** and develop as a group five to seven rules of engagement for the conversation.

Step 3: Practice and reflect on active listening. Although the ground rules set the tone for the conversation, establishing personal guidelines can help individuals focus their thoughts, feelings, and actions during dialogue. Building staff's self-awareness regarding how to be productive and active participants allows for a proactive stance that guards against potential downfalls. For example, having a personal guideline about active listening can help ensure that you hear and honor all voices during a conversation. This is key to keeping conversations moving forward, and forward movement requires what I call *progressive participation. Progressive* speaks to remaining open-minded throughout discussions, and *participation* refers to one's persistence, despite roadblocks, to actively listen, thereby securing deeper learning and understanding concerning others' experiences and feelings.

FIGURE 3.8

The ABCs of Conversations About Race

Acknowledge differences.	Never assume or make judgments.
Be willing to dig deeper.	Opting out is not an option.
Connect through lived experiences.	Practice patience.
Don't make it personal.	Question only for deeper understanding.
Expect and welcome discomfort.	Recognize bias.
Face the conversation head-on.	Speak from your perspective.
Generalizing is not fruitful.	Tame your tongue.
Honor another's honesty.	Understand mistakes will be made.
Invite other perspectives.	Verify your assumptions.
Justifying is not necessary.	Work as an equal conversation partner.
Know there are things you don't know.	X-ray your emotions (are your feelings getting in the way?)
Listen to learn.	You are not in a debate.
Monitor your body language.	Zoom in and clear your mind.

Here are some norms to consider:

- **Pay attention.** Listen intently to what people say. Don't take everything at face value, and search for deeper meaning and understanding. Monitor your tone and disposition, and recognize your personal feelings to guard against overreactions.
- **Pause.** After hearing others out, take a moment to think before responding. Give yourself a moment to ensure you heard or are understanding everything clearly.
- **Play it back.** When you pause, replay in your mind what you think you have just heard.
- **Paraphrase.** After you replay, paraphrase your understanding aloud to make sure you captured what the speaker feels are the key points or takeaways. Paraphrasing is a way to confirm your thinking and gain insight into your misconceptions because it gives the other person a chance to explain their words.

- **Persevere.** These conversations often start off feeling awkward, but working through discomfort and negative emotions can kickstart further understanding and learning. Take a moment to breathe, but don't shut down or opt out.

The activity in Figure 3.9 can help reinforce norms of active listening and progressive participation.

FIGURE 3.9
Setting Conversation Conditions: Activity 2

Format:
All-Staff Meeting (20–25 minutes)

Materials:
Copies of the Progressive Participation Reflection Form (Figure 3.10; download at www.ascd.org/EquityLeadershipHandouts) and a timer

Activity:
1. Display the five progressive participation attributes (pay attention, pause, playback, paraphrase, and persevere). Briefly review and discuss each with staff.

2. In pairs, have staff members set the timer and talk for one minute each in response to this prompt: "What worries me/makes me uncomfortable having conversations about race is...."

3. After the minute is up, the listener will practice using the rest of the participation attributes, seeking to pause, playback, and paraphrase what their partner shared while remembering to persevere.

4. Repeat the process with the speaker and listener roles switched.

5. After the second partner has shared, hand out the **Progressive Participation Reflection Form** for each member to fill out individually for personal reflection.

6. (Optional) After participants have filled out the reflection form, have pairs discuss what was easier or harder than expected.

Leadership teaching point: At the conclusion of the reflection time, share the following point: "This was just a snapshot of how to honor others in conversation. It will get easier the more we engage in discussion." Challenge staff to practice this skill and build it as a conscious habit. *Note:* Conduct this activity on a regular basis using different conversation starters to build a habit of effective listening.

The Progressive Participation Reflection Form shown in Figure 3.10, which is integral to the activity, supports participants as they reflect on what they have learned.

FIGURE 3.10
Progressive Participation Reflection Form

1. Circle the area(s) you feel went well. • Pay attention • Pause • Playback • Paraphrase • Persevere	What attributed to things going well?
2. Circle the area(s) you feel need work. • Pay attention • Pause • Playback • Paraphrase • Persevere	What attributed to things not going so well?
3. Rate your ability to **pay attention**, 5 being the highest rating. ← → 1 2 3 4 5	What did you notice about your tone, disposition, and feelings while listening?
4. Rate your ability to **persevere**, 5 being the highest rating. ← → 1 2 3 4 5	What deeper understanding did you gain?

LEADERSHIP TIP

When encouraging these conversations, pay attention to the racial dynamics among the participants. If there are educators of color on your staff, being aware of the following pitfalls—and taking corrective action as needed—can make all the difference:

- **"Historian syndrome."** Guard against placing people of color in a position of teaching their colleagues about the history and reality of racism. This casts them as responsible for others' progress toward embracing equity. As the leader, make sure the questions and conversations are not just directed to the expertise and experiences of the people of color in the room.

- **Exposure and retraumatization.** These conversations ask for a different level of vulnerability from nonwhite staff. For those who have been on the receiving end of racism, sharing their experiences can feel like opening the wounds of past trauma. This can be especially frustrating when they know that the white majority may simply not understand. Watch for comments—such as "Did that really happen?" or "Are you sure it was racism?"—that delegitimize someone's personal story.

- **Silence from the majority.** When staff of color speak their truth about their lived experiences with racism, their words may resonate with great passion and emotion. This can create situations in which those in the majority feel stifled to speak because they're unable to relate to the experience and they don't know how to respond. For people of color, this can be deflating. They're left to wonder if they said something offensive or if they overshared. As a leader, ensure that participants acknowledge or affirm what others may choose to share. If you come to any roadblocks, be honest and say something to the effect of "It seems as though we're struggling to find the right words to say. Let's talk about why."

- **"Rescuer syndrome."** Hearing the stories of people of color during these conversations can create guilt within those who are fortunate to never have experienced racism. The guilt they feel can, at times, lead to outbursts of emotion as they try to navigate their feelings. People of color might respond to these outward displays of emotion by consoling ("rescuing") those who are emotionally affected. For people of color, this means having to minimize their own experiences and feelings to prioritize the well-being of others in the conversation. As a leader, if you observe these behaviors, provide time to self-reflect. You might say, "Let's take a moment to pause and think about what we're feeling right now."

Let's turn now to the third *C,* consciousness.

Consciousness

The aim of contemplation and conversation is to develop consciousness. We accomplish this when we act on what we've learned to address inequality. The more we engage in conversations about race, the closer we should move toward this active level of consciousness. At this point, we embrace differences; instead of avoiding or ignoring present realities, we remain in constant pursuit of truth by bringing to light and rectifying circumstances dealing with injustice. We have come to the realization that there's a price we pay for our silence in that it staggers human potential, lowers productivity, and creates an increasing wave of fear (Tatum, 1997).

If the right conversations are happening, adults will move along a continuum toward a place of empowerment and consistent action. Let's look at this continuum, with its five levels of racial consciousness.

Level 1: Unenlightened. Being unenlightened means you don't believe that race influences the school environment. This doesn't indicate that a person's views or character are coming from a negative place. It's more about an inability to fully see the problem. These same individuals may acknowledge differences among racial groups, but they don't believe that race is a cause of those differences. Here are some of their common views:

- "I love all kids. I choose not to see color."
- "Race has no influence in our school environment."
- "It's about poverty and uninvolved parents, not color."
- "Our institution provides equal opportunity for all to succeed if individual students work hard enough."
- "Race only becomes an issue when we make it the focus."

Level 2: Powerless. Here, individuals acknowledge the reality of racial inequality but feel powerless because they see these inequities as a product of a faulty system that they didn't create. They may find conversations about race frustrating because they think they're doing the right things in not being part of the problem and have little power to change the system or influence others. Here are some views you may encounter:

- "Our students of color *are* spending more time in the office, but we need to hold parents accountable and get consistency from home."
- "If some adults are having issues with race, it's the job of leadership to detect the problem and deal with those individuals directly."
- "We *are* having issues closing the achievement gap, but students come to us behind academically, and we're constantly playing catch-up."
- "We lack the resources to meet the needs of our students of color."

Level 3: Awakening. Here, people slowly begin to see the role that they or other educators can play in helping to reduce the negative influences of race. Although they tend to shy away from the larger conversation to avoid confrontation, they're willing to openly discuss the topic in smaller groups when those they trust initiate the conversation. Individuals in this phase still question the power of their voice in influencing change, but they are committed to making sure they're not exasperating the problem. The views they express look like this:

- "At times, students in our building get treated differently because of race."
- "I have seen others display biases that contribute to disparities."
- "Some of our practices don't seem to benefit all our students."
- "I stay away from negative individuals and situations of injustice."
- "I remain positive and check myself to make sure that I'm not placing students in disparaging situations."

Level 4: Intuitive. Here, adults are clearly beginning to put the pieces together. These individuals recognize their race-associated positional freedom (or lack of it), and they realize they may hold biases or act in ways they're unaware of. They're willing to take part in conversations or actions regarding racial inequalities, but they're not comfortable taking the lead. They seek to educate themselves about the effects of race and to understand any role their thoughts, actions, or position might play. They may hold some of the following views:

- "I recognize systemic conditions that are holding back others, admittedly sometimes after the fact, but I struggle to identify what the next steps might be to help influence change."
- "I understand the importance of having conversations about race that question the status quo, but I'm not sure how to help others become comfortable."
- "When invited, I'm willing to engage in discussions about race with those outside my circle."
- "I understand that I'm unaware of some aspects of race and that part of the solution is my becoming aware of this fact."

Level 5: Action-Oriented. These individuals actively seek to be aware of implications with race and work to influence change. They monitor their own actions, positional freedoms, and behaviors and are willing to engage in conversations that ask deeper questions to advocate for change. They also understand that being an advocate for equity means confronting all aspects within the environment that hinder the formation of equity. They tend to hold the following beliefs:

- "I'm beginning to understand who I am and how race is contributing to systemic conditions of institutional racism."
- "It only takes one small voice to make a difference, and my silence will only contribute to the problem."
- "It's my duty to speak up when students or others are suffering injustice."
- "We must hold ourselves accountable and focus on our span of control."
- "I seek to understand my positional freedom and to leverage it to positively affect change."

When schools achieve an action-oriented level of consciousness, adults are functioning as *educational equity allies,* commonly welcoming accountability and constructive discomfort. The culture isn't committed to everyone just getting along; it's committed to creating the degree of discomfort necessary to ensure that the environment addresses the needs of all. Equitable circumstances will not transpire unless allies provide a crucial level of awareness and support. When educators take bold action and assume the role of educational equity allies, they lighten the burdens associated with being a student of color. Educators not only become aware of the institutional struggles of students of color but also take advantage of the gravity of the moment by becoming an advocate for change. It's important to stay committed to the processes of *contemplation* and *conversation* to build both the will and skill to *consciously* act on needed change.

LEADERSHIP TIP

Don't feel overwhelmed about having to get staff to the action-oriented stage. Ensuing chapters in this book will help you guide staff to this state. Take it one day at a time, and know that change will not happen overnight. Most important, stay committed to the process.

Making the Most of Time

Getting conversations about race off the ground will take dedicated efforts and strategies. You'll need to consider which organizational structures you can leverage to support effective dialogue. To move adults out of their cultural bubbles (Ross, 2013), they will need time during professional opportunities to build heightened awareness of race. Consider the school structures shown in Figure 3.11 as you plan discussion opportunities for staff.

FIGURE 3.11
Six Structures That Support a Culture of Constructive Discomfort

1. **Virtual learning groups.** Using a virtual platform is a viable option when there are challenges to bringing staff together for in-person dialogue. Although this allows for flexibility, virtual meetings cannot re-create all areas of human interaction. Given this fact, you will want to be thoughtful about the norms and conditions required for an inclusive virtual conversation.

2. **Staff meetings.** Structure equity conversation time during each staff meeting. This builds a habit of practice, and being intentional in this way supports the reflective practice and growth of staff.

3. **Teacher common planning time.** Help teachers establish norms and protocols for conversations pertaining to equity and race when collaboratively planning for instruction.

4. **Professional learning communities.** In professional learning communities, participants can leverage data by establishing goals that create an intentional focus on equity and race. This is also a great opportunity for staff to review professional material to expand their knowledge of the best instructional approaches.

5. **Workshops.** In full- or half-day workshops, school leaders can dive deeper into conversations and topics. This is also an opportune time to assess staff buy-in or refocus staff on the mission and vision.

6. **Coaching/evaluation.** Engaging in discussions about race and equity can be a fruitful part of the coaching and evaluation process. It can support personal accountability and increase awareness of inequitable practices.

Next Steps for Leaders: Narrow Your Focus

Before diving into a deeper exploration of how to create a comfortably uncomfortable environment, it's important to recognize leadership approaches that will derail this process. Success will depend on your ability to be on the lookout for three mindsets—ones highlighted in Jeremy Gutsche's *Better and Faster* (2015) as key for business leaders: *not too big, not too small,* and *not what you know.*

Let's look at these ideas in the context of the focus, competence, and passion we need to achieve equity.

"Not too big." Every good idea or strategy isn't always good for you. It's important to consider the size and pace of the change. Introducing too many big ideas and strategies can be overwhelming or hyper-focus people on the size of the task. As you get started, dig deep into each idea or strategy and search for opportunities that match the current level of readiness and the talents of staff.

"Not too small." Don't think so small or move so slowly that the conversation loses its luster and fades away. Generating a long-lasting effect on student learning outcomes will require steps that are *sizable* enough along the way. Taking overly small steps can send the message that we're not completely invested in the change, and it can heighten frustration.

"Not what you know." Avoid spending too much time leaning on strategies you've already tried. These strategies and ideas will pop out at you because of the brain's innate tendency to farm the same ground, but if these approaches didn't bear fruit previously, they may not be worth further investment. And don't think you need to adopt every suggestion in this book lockstep; select the strategies that satisfy your needs and develop additional strategies of your own.

Ask yourself...
- To what extent have we established a collaborative culture within the environment?
- What are the first steps I plan to take to build staff capacity for conversations about race?
- How will I hold myself accountable to staying grounded in leading this equity work while keeping "not too big," "not too small," and "not what you know" in mind?

4

Building Efficacy

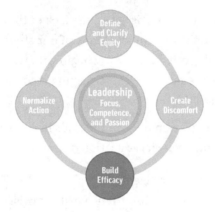

*"An important leverage point for transforming our
education system is changing the mindset
that gave rise to it in the first place."*

—Todd Rose, *The End of Average*

Although a system can reach equity through a procedural approach, it's not as simple as just checking off boxes with each completed step. As with most waves that arise in education, mindsets matter; they can aid or prohibit a shifting of the tide.

Consider a conversation between an elementary school principal and two of his teachers following a grade-level meeting in which participants examined student performance data:

Teacher 1: We'd really like to discuss the grade-level meeting that took place this morning. We don't know if you meant any harm, but it felt like you were telling us that we aren't working hard enough to teach our minority students.

Principal: I'm sorry you feel that way. To help me understand, can you be more specific about your frustrations?

Teacher 2: Well, it just feels like we're always being asked to do more, but we fail to discuss the real challenges we face.

Teacher 1: What she's saying is, given the lack of time we have to actually teach, we can only do so much. Many of our students are so behind that we're challenged by where to even begin with the curriculum. We're asked to do more one-on-one with struggling students, but where does that leave the rest of the class?

Teacher 2: Not to mention the fact that kids have to *want* to learn, and most of us don't hold a special education degree.

Although the teachers are clearly speaking out of frustration, the message subtly communicated behind their words is this: *We just don't know if we have what it takes to make a difference.*

The Power of Belief

Walk the hallways of a school struggling with belief, and you'll pick up on a similar tone of exhaustion and defeat from staff charged with raising the achievement levels of students of color. What is the source of their struggle? A deficiency of efficacy.

In this context, *efficacy* pertains to the perception educators hold that their efforts will have a positive effect on student learning (Goddard et al., 2000). A low efficacy level has an uncanny way of generating thoughts leading to actions that create disparity. Efficacy influences how students acquire knowledge, how people deal with events, what kind of behavior they model, how the system allocates resources, and what people pay attention to and reward (Schein, 1992). To produce equitable outcomes, it's crucial, as part of the Equity Leadership Framework, to build efficacy within staff both individually and collectively.

Before we go any further, let's try a simple exercise. On a blank piece of paper, draw a T-chart (make a large letter *T* that covers the length of the paper). Write "Low Efficacy" at the top of one column and "High Efficacy" at the top of the other. Now, thinking about the staff in your building, place the names of those you believe meet a particular level of efficacy in the appropriate column. After completing this step, brainstorm a list of general characteristics that land individuals in one of these two categories. For example, evidence of high efficacy might be openness to new ideas, patience when working with challenging students, and strong organization and planning. Evidence of low efficacy might include reluctance to try new approaches, a tendency to blame outside factors for negative outcomes, and frequent frustration. Now look at your lists, and ask yourself what *beliefs* might lie behind the characteristics on each side of the T-chart.

According to Pajares (1992), teachers' beliefs about their teaching abilities are a key indicator of their behavior, including the decisions they make and how they organize their classroom environments. A higher degree of adult efficacy is therefore a crucial factor in eradicating systemic challenges and getting to equity. In fact, the academic disparity we see for students of color may have more to do with teacher efficacy than with student aptitude.

The classic Pygmalion experiment conducted by researchers Robert Rosenthal and Lenore Jacobson (1968) in a public-school setting shows how easily beliefs can sway equity. The experiment centered on an intelligence test that Rosenthal and Jacobson called "the Harvard Test of Inflected Acquisition." The researchers wished to see to what degree teacher expectations contributed to higher rates of failure among lower-class and minority students. The teachers in the study worked in a primarily lower-class community. They were led to believe that the test could determine not only student IQ but also the speed of intellectual progress that each student would make in a single year. At the start of school, students took the acquisition test, and teachers then received a list of students they could expect to succeed in their classroom based on the students' individual test scores. What Rosenthal and Jacobson didn't disclose, however, was that the students on the lists were randomly selected; the difference in aptitude between the two groups of students—those on the "success" lists and those who were not—was solely in the minds of the teachers.

Before the end of the school year, the students took a second intelligence test. The researchers wanted to see what had transpired, given the "expected" rapid growth in performance for the selected students. What they found was that, on average, the students identified for rapid academic growth had an increase of more than 12 points on their IQ scores compared with the 8-point increase among the remaining students in each class. Rosenthal and Jacobson found that identified students in grades 1 and 2 were experiencing increases of 20 points or more on their IQ scores and enjoyed more praise from their teachers. In addition, teachers described the students who were labeled with the potential for rapid growth as better behaved, more academically curious, possessing greater opportunity for future success, and friendlier when compared with other students. The researchers also noted that the teachers were more enthusiastic about teaching the identified students; they were warmer and spent additional time with them.

What do the results of this study say about efficacy? That the amount of effort expended assuredly influences the capability of those on the receiving end. The uneven experiences that underserved students encounter throughout their educational journey too often reflect lower levels of efficacy on the part of educators. When asking Black students about external factors that influenced their education, Kati Haycock (2001) found that students pointed out factors related to adult efficacy:

> They talk about teachers who often do not know the subjects that they are teaching. They talk about counselors who consistently underestimate their potential and place them in lower-level courses. They talk about principals who dismiss their concerns. And they talk about a curriculum and a set of expectations that feel so miserably low level that they literally bore the students right out the school door. (p. 8)

LEADERSHIP TIP

A word of caution here. Although teacher efficacy is clearly a factor in getting to equity, leaders need to remember that teachers are not the sole source of the equity problem. Positioning them as such undermines the need to examine systemic factors or other root causes that replicate educational inequities for students of color (García & Guerra, 2004). If teachers struggle with efficacy, they may work in unsupportive conditions, have ineffective leadership, and lack the training and resources they need. Leaders should reflect on whether they're removing barriers and creating pathways to success for teachers.

Lower Expectations = Lower Efficacy

The belief gap is generally attributed to risk factors that teachers may associate with students of color, such as lower socioeconomic status, more aggressive behaviors, family structures that are unsupportive of school and learning, or lack of focus and motivation. Some educators view these conditions as bigger than themselves; as a result, they may develop a sense of helplessness regarding their ability to educate. Other well-intentioned educators embrace a savior mentality, characterized by seeking to protect students of color from harm.

Unfortunately, both approaches result in an all-too-familiar educational tale. As Haycock (2001) notes, educators may be moved to give these students "less of everything that we believe makes a difference" (p. 8). Rachel, a high school English teacher, recounted for me how she struggled with efficacy and at-risk students early on in her teaching journey:

> I can remember feeling frustrated that I was asked to teach content I knew minority students in my classroom could not handle. The material was two grade levels above their learning and ignored the many challenges outside the school setting that made it impossible for them to learn. I did my best to care for them and give them everything I could. I would walk by classrooms and see teachers berating students or sitting at their desks while lecturing. I vowed I was going to be different. I tutored students before and after the school day, made parent phone calls, and many days offered students opportunity during my plan time to come for assistance.
>
> It was not until my 5th year, when I met Darius, that I realized that my students were not the problem. It was my struggle with belief. All those years, I had been "protecting" students from failure. Giving them work that they could "handle." Asking questions that didn't require deep thinking to not cause embarrassment.
>
> Darius changed everything. He observed the way I interacted with other students who did not look like him. He noticed the expectations were different and that those students were never asked to do less. One day while tutoring Darius, he asked me an honest question I will never

forget. "Ms. Rachel, if you care about me and my learning, why do you treat me different?"

"What do you mean?" I asked. He replied, "I notice that I never seem to get asked to work as hard as the white students in class. You ask them most of the questions and give me less work." My heart sank. He was right. Darius could never do better because my actions communicated that I never really expected him to do better. My version of care was not the only care he needed. Darius needed a teacher who believed in his ability to help him rise to the challenge, not live to a lower standard. (Personal communication, February 1, 2018)

The important takeaway here is that low efficacy is not always operating with negative intent. Rachel wanted what was best for Darius, but her beliefs obstructed her ability to provide him with the best instruction. When diverse students face perceived at-risk factors, adults may unconsciously focus more on the need for care and less on the need for learning (García & Guerra, 2004). Consequently, underserved students will experience instructional practices that inadvertently reflect a *pedagogy of inequality*.

Figure 4.1 shows the methods and practices that ensue from such an approach. Reflect on each of the low-expectancy practices listed in the figure. Which ones have you observed in your school?

FIGURE 4.1

A Pedagogy of Inequality

• Few opportunities for students to turn and talk with peers	• Slower teacher pacing
• Teachers rescuing students too soon when they struggle with problem solving	• Lower-level questions (e.g., yes/no questions) overrepresented
• Little wait time offered	• Not asking students to explain their thinking
• Little specific feedback provided	• Teacher lecturing/carrying academic load
• More punitive consequences for social behavior, as opposed to reteaching	• Less risk taking and more handholding during instruction
• Overuse of worksheets	• Less positive affirmation
• Lower levels of academic accountability	• Few opportunities for productive struggle
• Little patience with academic struggles	• Little guided questioning
• Engaging students in craft activities as part of learning, as opposed to more rigorous assignments	• Overuse of computer programs to teach students

Given that students of color are more likely to encounter lower expectations (Ferguson, 2000; Weinstein, 2002), leaders need to be aware of the various levels of teacher efficacy in their schools. The practices listed in Figure 4.1 are ones to watch for. Although educators may genuinely assert that they love all children, treat all students fairly, and never do emotional harm, their actions may speak louder than their words.

Efficacy is more important in explaining school achievement than socioeconomic status (Hoy et al., 2002). Low levels of efficacy can further extenuate at-risk factors. For example, for students of color, experiencing gaps in belief leads not only to inequity but also to learned helplessness. In *The New Jim Crow: Mass Incarceration in the Age of Colorblindness*, Michelle Alexander (2012) points out that as a result of educational inequity, culturally diverse students may become dependent learners. What these students need are instructional practices that target equity through learner independence. And teachers are more likely to resort to such practices when school leaders support them in holding high expectations for all their students.

The Importance of Collective Efficacy

In *Good to Great*, Jim Collins (2001) dispels the notion that people are the most important asset in an organization; what really matters is having the *right* people. As the saying goes, "It takes teamwork to make the dream work." Getting to equity won't happen unless people believe not only in themselves but also in the capability of their colleagues. Now, focusing on self-efficacy doesn't preclude some highly effective teachers from congregating with other highly effective teachers in pockets of effective silos—pockets surrounded by less effective colleagues.

To establish collective efficacy across the board, leaders need to help the adults in their building believe in one another. Collective efficacy enables adults to work competently in an environment where they perceive they're supported and where they trust in a common goal. In such environments, adults confidently face challenges, comprehend that they can accomplish more by working together, and view themselves as an important part of a whole. They welcome collaborative practice, work together to solve complex student problems, and effectively leverage group and individual accountability to create change. When leaders create environments with strong levels of collective efficacy, people commit to putting in the time and effort to meet diverse needs, setting challenging goals, and making necessary personal and teaching adjustments. Consequently, students of color in such environments not only perceive their teachers' confidence in their ability to learn but also sense that adults truly care about them (Collier, 2005). A sense of care translates into better academic outcomes because students tend to work harder for teachers who communicate concern for their well-being.

Collective efficacy is the number one factor influencing equitable educational outcomes within the classroom (Hattie, 2012). Efficacy is infectious within a learning environment, and leaders should help staff comprehend that we tend to get out of it what we put in. This is not to suggest that positive results will come easily. But efficacy certainly influences adult motivation and the desire to do what it takes. When leaders facilitate cultures of strong efficacy, they can transform the academic and social outcomes of students of color. Research shows the following benefits in such cultures:

- Teachers tend to implement instructional practices at more of a master level. Students at lower levels of progression have a teacher who works with them with persistence and resiliency (Tschannen-Moran & Barr, 2004).
- Teachers carry higher expectations (Bandura, 1997), and they convey this by keeping their composure with students who make mistakes (Ashton & Webb, 1986).
- Teachers find productive ways to deal with problem behavior (Gibbs & Powell, 2011).
- Teachers become more willing to integrate new strategies (Parks et al., 2007).
- The extent of teacher leadership grows, increasing the focus on assisting others and actively sharing ideas (Derrington & Angelle, 2013).

Each of these advantages speaks to the value of aiding a culture to embrace higher efficacy.

Building a Culture of Efficacy

With all that emerges throughout the course of the day, it can be challenging for leaders to build and maintain high levels of efficacy among staff. In a candid conversation I had with a high school principal, he shared how cumbersome this challenge can be:

> It literally keeps me up at night. It's extremely hard to alter the minds of adults who are so set in their ways. We are constantly talking about having a growth mindset and the effect of fixed beliefs, but I cannot force teachers to change.

Building efficacy may be a struggle, but it is doable. Despite that principal feeling he had little control, he is the biggest factor influencing the development of efficacy among his teachers. First, leaders set the conditions for teacher success. Second, they can provide emotional support and remove barriers that prohibit teachers' ability to evolve. Leaders exhibit high-efficacy leadership when they build the appropriate level of belief or confidence within the environment. Such leaders do the following:

- **Neutralize weakness.** Lower efficacy results in deficit ideologies. Leaders must conscientiously monitor the environment to detect shortfalls with efficacy or problems with adult emotional well-being. By doing so, they can neutralize any negative effects by encouraging thoughts and actions in line with high-efficacy approaches.
- **Sow optimism.** Leaders must inspire a sense of purpose and hope for the future within the organization. They can do so by setting benchmarks and goals that provide immediate value, leveraging leadership presence, empowering others, and strengthening collaborative practice.
- **Support growth.** Never forget the power of personal connection. When staff members feel that their leaders consistently support and care for them, it boosts their level of confidence. Such leaders show a willingness to serve and the ability to empathize at the appropriate time.

LEADERSHIP TIP

Part of the challenge of building efficacy is that staff members have varying personalities and hold a range of beliefs. Understand the power you possess as a leader. Spend time reflecting on your approach to high-efficacy leadership. To build the efficacy of others, you will have to model both your expectations and beliefs.

Let's now take a closer look at the three steps leaders can take to elevate the level of efficacy within a culture.

Step 1: Neutralize Weakness

When adults exhibit desirable thoughts and behaviors, a leader enhances a school culture by not disrupting them. However, in the absence of such behaviors, a leader's inaction is detrimental to the pursuits of coherence and equity. Although being an effective leader is not about micromanaging, something does take place within the soul of a culture each time leaders overlook or ignore undesirable events.

Let me share a multi-part scenario as illustration.

Anthony, a 4th grader in an inner-city school, is struggling to learn. He lives with three younger siblings in a single-parent household and has limited contact with his father. His mother is frequently unavailable to meet with the school because she works two jobs to make ends meet.

Anthony's kindergarten teacher was the first to note that although Anthony appeared eager to learn, he struggled to meet expectations. As the years passed, his elementary school teachers continued to note his lack of focus and seeming inability to follow classroom rules. The early, hopeful notes about Anthony's enthusiasm were replaced with observations that he seemed unwilling to try.

Now, in Anthony's 4th grade year, his behavior is consistently noncompliant, his academics continue to slip, and he's becoming more detached from school. The school has labeled Anthony an at-risk child, and they have begun testing him for special education.

Question: What conclusions can you draw about Anthony and his ability to learn?

At Anthony's school, the majority of teachers come from a middle-class background. They spend most of their time in front of the classroom, where they can best keep an eye on student interactions. They teach the curriculum straight from the teacher resource book, and they assign students the accompanying lower-level activities for independent practice. When the teachers engage in small-group instruction, they carry the cognitive load when questioning students' thinking. The teachers feel pressed to keep up with the pacing guide, so they stick to what is required, which leaves little time to truly connect with students. The principal of the building is usually in his office handling discipline issues or doing paperwork.

Question: *Keeping in mind the information you have learned about Anthony's history, what conclusions have you now drawn about Anthony's ability to learn?*

It's important to step back and think about the big picture. During Anthony's first few weeks of kindergarten, his face would light up with excitement as he looked around the classroom and observed all the things they had at school to do. He loved to draw and was fascinated by the colored paints and markers in the art center. Anthony was full of energy and frequently sought to share a story or thought with his teacher or classmates during the day. His voice always seemed to be the loudest in the classroom, and if something exciting was happening, he was always right there.

Anthony's kindergarten teacher, who was in her seventh year of teaching at the time, was known for keeping an orderly classroom. After the first few months of school, she found herself frustrated with Anthony and his propensity to talk. His chattiness was interfering with other students' ability to learn, and he struggled to stay in his seat. "This one is going to be a handful," she told her colleagues. Anthony came in lacking several key skills (she confirmed that he had had no formal early childhood education), and she gauged that support from home would be difficult because his mom had three other children to think about.

The kindergarten teacher's interactions with Anthony followed a predictable pattern of telling him what he was doing wrong. Because of his "erratic behavior," he found himself isolated from the rest of the class in a seat at the front of the room. To get the teacher's attention, Anthony would ask lots of questions about how to do an assignment and would walk back to his seat defeated when the teacher would tell him, in her best teacher voice, that he would have to wait his turn. On the occasions he persisted in asking questions, he found himself barred from recess and had to stay inside to do classwork. Daily, classmates accused Anthony of something, whether he was the instigator or not, and the more he pleaded his case, the deeper he found himself in trouble.

Question: *Keeping in mind all you have now learned about Anthony's school experience, what final conclusions do you draw about Anthony's ability to learn?*

Although there are many rationales as to why Anthony is not on track for success, it's clear how the school environment failed to improve his circumstances. This example also illustrates why labels such as *at risk* can easily become a self-fulfilling prophecy. As the years went by, Anthony internalized this negative label that the school had given him and gave his teachers the exact behavior they expected to see.

Collective efficacy cannot thrive in environments where no one challenges these types of labels and feelings. Words matter. They operate on a subconscious level and easily can become ingrained in a school's psyche. Because thoughts carry immense power, leaders must be decisive in deconstructing undesired thinking. A commitment to developing an anti-deficit culture enables you, as a leader, to neutralize weakness by building on adult emotional well-being, thus supporting greater efficacy.

There are two crucial aspects to neutralizing weakness: (1) understanding environmental struggles and (2) reframing deficit thinking.

Understanding environmental struggles. Start by looking for the pedagogies of inequality highlighted in Figure 4.1 (see p. 64). Pay attention to how adults respond to challenges in the environment. The Efficacy Barriers chart shown in Figure 4.2 lists dispositions you may encounter, among both staff and school leaders, when people struggle with efficacy.

Reframing deficit thinking. Take steps to address deficit thoughts and actions to secure more positive approaches and outlooks. Here is what I recommend:

- **Examine language use buildingwide.** Work with staff to identify terms that reinforce inferiority, and develop an alternative common language to strengthen the environment. Questions to ask include the following:
  - —Does this language add value (asset)?
  - —For whom does it add value, and how?
  - —Do aspects of this language diminish (deficit) groups? How?
  - —What language can we use that supports emotional well-being?

- **Purposefully address lower levels of adult efficacy.** This doesn't mean leading through micromanagement. In Figure 4.3, you will find leadership stances for dealing with various lower-efficacy mentalities

---

FIGURE 4.2

Efficacy Barriers: Teacher and Leader Dispositions

Teacher Dispositions

- **Self-justifying.** It's never quite the teacher's fault. There always seems to be a defensible explanation for why they're unable to meet students' academic needs (for example, "I don't know what they were taught last year").
- **Frequent frustration.** The sky always appears to be falling. Conversations regularly start with what's wrong with students, as opposed to talking about strengths. Even when teachers observe strengths, they tend to believe those strengths will be short-lived.
- **"I have everything figured out."** Teachers don't welcome feedback or want to collaborate about strategies because they believe they are doing their best and have tried all those other things that everyone suggested and found they didn't work.
- **Fear.** Teachers are fearful about not being able to implement strategies correctly or get through to students.

Leader Dispositions

- **Self-justifying.** It's never quite the leader's fault. There always seems to be a defensible explanation for why they can't move staff toward positive change (for example, "They're all adults; they have to *want* to change").
- **Frequent frustration.** The sky always appears to be falling. Conversations about staff regularly start with things that aren't happening in the building. People who are doing the right thing are commonly overlooked.
- **"I have everything figured out."** Leaders don't welcome feedback or input from staff. The general feeling is that if people just did what they were told, things would work out.
- **Fear.** Leaders make decisions based on the thoughts and actions of staff who "make the most noise."

---

and practices. Here are a few important things to consider when applying each stance:

—When delivering a difficult message, do it with care.

—Don't forget to be a listener. Listening builds trust and communicates care. It also enables us to truly comprehend the desires and needs of others.

—Search for balance. Even those who need tough love should have opportunities to teach and learn in more effective ways and receive your affirmation for doing so.

- **Coach staff in reframing deficit ideologies.** When you observe staff struggling with deficit thinking, facilitate a process of problem solving to help them get to a space of ideal reasoning.

FIGURE 4.3

Leadership Stances for Dealing with Lower-Efficacy Practices

- **A touch of reality.** Some individuals will need help gaining a realistic perspective of what's happening. When going through the motions of "been there, done that," these individuals might benefit from a frequent dose of what I call the Dr. Phil question: *How's that working for you?*
- **Tough love.** For individuals who refuse to move, you may need to increase your presence to show you're not going anywhere. Communicate that you are invested in their success, and set clear parameters and expectations for growth.
- **Teaching and learning.** Some people will do better once they know better. They're operating on what they know and believe works, but once they're shown a better way, they will find success.
- **Collaborative reflection.** Some need a thought partner to help them examine what is working or not working within the classroom. Offer an extra pair of eyes and ears to highlight what is going well, and provide a nudge where growth opportunities exist.
- **Support.** Some individuals just need someone there to catch them when they fall. As they try new strategies, it will be helpful for them to be observed, to reflect, and to receive timely feedback.
- **Affirmation.** Some individuals need permission to step outside their comfort zones. By assuring them of your belief in their abilities, they will learn to trust the process to achieve desired outcomes.
- **Acknowledgment.** Some individuals just need to be recognized. Pointing out their effort and good intentions will help open doors to learning better practices.

Watzlawick and colleagues (1974) define *reframing* as "changing the conceptual and/or emotional setting or viewpoint in relation to which a situation is experienced and to place it in another frame which fits the 'facts' of the same concrete situation equally well or even better, and thereby changing its entire meaning" (p. 95).

Use the guide shown in Figure 4.4 to coach individual staff members through deficit thoughts to create new meaning or replacement thoughts. You will find a blank form for use with your staff in the Appendix's Tool B.

Let's return to the scenario set at the beginning of the chapter: a principal meeting with two teachers discouraged by students' performance. Figure 4.5 shows how a leader might use the guide with staff to reframe their thinking; that is, it shows how Teacher 2 might have completed the Confronting Deficit Thinking Guide shown in Figure 4.4.

> **Principal:** Thank you for stopping in. I'd like to follow up on the conversation we had earlier in my office. I sensed your frustration and wanted to dig a little deeper to see if I can help.

Teacher 2: Well, OK, but I shared everything I wanted to say.

Principal: I understand. I just want to explore a comment you made. You mentioned that "students have to *want* to learn." As a staff, we've been discussing how reframing our thinking can lead to positive outlooks and outcomes. I'd like to use that reframing model to work through your thinking in order to figure out what we might do to turn things around.

FIGURE 4.4
Confronting Deficit Thinking Guide

Write a statement recording what you're currently grappling with.

Discovery Process	Reframing Process
Assessing • Describe the emotional reaction this thought is causing. How is it affecting your words and actions? • What are you hoping that others will understand by communicating this thought?	**Reassessing** • As you examine this thought, what words do you need to remove/replace to shift your thinking to a positive light? *(Think about biases and assumptions that are not based on facts and thus are taking you down a negative path.)*
Examining Hidden Bias • Thinking about your experiences as opposed to those of your students or their families, what advantages can you identify? Consider the following: —Family structure —Socioeconomic status (home life) —Classroom experience (learning, behavior, representation, relationships) • What might your personal experiences be leading you to believe what you currently believe or see? • What biases or stereotypes might you be holding? • How might this thinking be perpetuating a systemic or preexisting narrative?	**Building a Future State** • What personal biases do you need to confront to view this from an honest and a realistic perspective? • What actions could you take to build positive momentum? • What replacement thoughts might make your thinking more useful by creating a new narrative or personal experience? *(Replace the word or words you removed in the box above with those that communicate optimism.)*

Write a reconstructed thought (think proactive) using the replacement words/ thoughts.

The leader sets the stage for further problem solving by guiding staff members through the following steps to complete the form:

- Establish the deficit thought. (As shown in Figure 4.5, the deficit thought is "Kids have to want to learn.")
- Guide the staff member by working through the discovery process shown in the left-hand column of the guide. This involves assessing the problem and then searching for hidden bias.
- After exploring underlying thoughts and feelings, the staff member engages in the reframing process, as shown in the right-hand column of the guide. This involves reassessing the original thought (the *have to* in "Kids have to want to learn") and building a positive future state.
- Have the staff member reconstruct a new thought to help build positive and proactive thinking. In this case, the staff member wrote down this reconstructed thought: "The students will learn if I make learning relevant to them."

LEADERSHIP TIP

To change the culture, you will have to guide staff members who struggle with deficit thinking. This can feel like a heavy burden, but understand this: *What you permit, you promote.* It's not about being confrontational but about finding a way to break the cycle for individuals who struggle. Deficit thinking affects your teachers' ability to have a positive effect on their students, and, in many cases, it leads to unfavorable or inequitable learning experiences. There is no way for you to police the whole environment; the goal is to exhibit the kind of leadership that encourages an environment committed to policing itself.

Step 2: Sow Optimism

In seeking to create higher levels of efficacy, leaders should consider moves that promote a sense of togetherness in the cause of equity. Here are some ways to increase levels of efficacy.

Leverage your presence. Every school leader is also a team member—one with an outsized influence when it comes to building trust and providing opportunities to celebrate success. Effective leaders influence staff through accountability laced with care. They show appreciation, lay a clear path of purpose, entrust others with autonomy, and recognize the good work of others.

Question: Where and when during the school day might you leverage your presence?

FIGURE 4.5

Confronting Deficit Thinking Guide: A Completed Sample

Write a statement recording what you are currently grappling with.
Kids have to want to learn.

Discovery Process	Reframing Process
Assessing • I'm feeling frustrated that we're to blame for our students' underperformance. • It feels like our efforts aren't recognized. • It's exhausting to feel like you're doing your best for students, only to see negative results. • I hope you understand that I'm doing the best I can.	**Reassessing** "have to"
Examining Hidden Bias • My family struggled with finances, but my parents expected me to do well in school. • I had teachers who were strict about learning. I always showed respect by doing what they told me to do. • My parents always communicated with my teachers. • Saying that students have to *want* to learn could be implying that students of color are unmotivated.	**Building a Future State** • I need to stop thinking that my students are making the choice not to learn. • I'm frustrated by the lack of support from home, but it's not helpful to assume that a lack of communication means a lack of care. • I just need help managing the wide range of learning abilities in my classroom. • Students have the ability to learn. I just need to find what works for them.

Write a reconstructed thought (think proactive) using the replacement words/ thoughts.

The students will learn if I make learning relevant to them.

Focus on quick wins. Although long-range goals are important in building higher levels of efficacy, it's equally important to focus on wins that generate measurable improvement in a short amount of time (Schmoker, 1999). Recognizing quick wins enables teachers to tear down deficit thoughts about change because they see that things are quickly moving in the right direction. Experiencing success intensifies motivation and positive thought processes and increases the likelihood that staff members will stick with future strategies.

Question: Based on your weaknesses with efficacy as a school (or district), in what areas do you need to generate short-term goals and quick wins?

Empower your staff. Leaders cannot accomplish the complex work of establishing equity on their own. Take active measures to establish a united front through shared leadership. Showing confidence in staff builds trust, cohesion, and a mutual sense of accountability. Think about how you're soliciting staff voices and empowering them to help carry the load. Conceding power shows staff that you value their thinking and that you understand they serve a vital role in reaching goals.

Question: Based on your observed weaknesses with efficacy as a school (or district), in what ways do you need to empower staff?

Provide time for collaborative practice. Enabling teachers to work together can raise their perception of the competence of their peers. Collaborative practice not only helps teachers overcome the negative effects of challenging building circumstances (Zambo & Zambo, 2008) but also builds reflection and willingness to help those in need of support.

Question: Based on your observed weaknesses with efficacy as a school (or district), how can you build on collaborative practice?

Step 3: Support Growth

Effective leaders understand that every leadership move that is not aligned with the stated purpose of moving toward equity is a setback for the culture. Staff members need to feel that they are part of the process. Work alongside staff, be in tune with their thoughts and feelings, communicate a clear mission, and implement appropriate levels of accountability.

Question: Based on your observed weaknesses with efficacy as a school (or district), how can you model effective support for staff?

Making the Most of Time

The truth is, every child is "at risk" when placed in environments in which adults hold negative beliefs about that child's potential. Schools that are effective in bridging the gap move beyond the implications of race and hold a strong shared belief that they possess the knowledge and skills to make a positive difference in the lives of diverse students—and that their actions reflect this commitment. By taking the time to support staff as they come to the realization that, collectively, they can help all students succeed, you will foster a caring culture that holds high expectations for students and that feels accountable for delivering quality education to all.

We can debate why students of color suffer academically; we can even argue the multiple reasons behind the struggle to meet their diverse needs. But here is where we draw the line: *If all these circumstances are insurmountable, why do we even bother to educate?* It's because there's a sliver of hope buried within our minds that educators hold immense power over circumstance. We know it's possible to reverse disparaging outcomes in achievement among underserved students whom others have given up on. This happens when leaders take the time to generate a high-efficacy culture that dispels the myth that students of color are "incapable of anything but low outcomes" (Johnson, 2002, p. 11).

The activity shown in Figure 4.6 is one way to get quick initial thoughts on collective efficacy beliefs within your environment. The I Believe Survey shown in Figure 4.7 is an integral part of that activity. The intent of both is for leaders and their staff to begin to learn how the current mindset is affecting change.

Next Steps for Leaders: Lead the Way

As Gandhi famously wrote, "Be the change you wish to see in the world." School leadership is the single most important factor in eliminating deficit ideologies within the school. It's therefore the single most important factor affecting the achievement of minority students (Parrett & Budge, 2012). If you want your staff to change, the work starts with you. Set conditions that enable staff to grow. As educator Ron Edmonds (1979) noted, "We can, wherever and whenever we choose, successfully teach all children whose schooling is of interest to us" (p. 23); the operative words here are "choose" and "interest." Lead in a way that encourages teachers to choose to rise to the occasion and do whatever it takes to effectively educate all the students in their charge.

Ask yourself...

- What next steps should I take in my environment to understand the current culture around efficacy?
- How and in what specific areas do I exhibit high-efficacy leadership?
- How should I work with individuals showing signs of lower efficacy?

FIGURE 4.6
Staff Belief Activity

Format
Staff meeting, 30–40 minutes

Materials
I Believe Survey (Figure 4.7; download at www.ascd.org/EquityLeadershipHandouts)

Activity
1. Give each staff member the **I Believe Survey** form and ask them to anonymously fill it out before the meeting. (Alternatively, staff members could fill out the form at the meeting, but note that this will require more time.)
2. Collect the responses and tally the results to share with staff.
3. Display the results for staff to see, or place copies of the results at each table.
4. Have staff in small groups (3–4 members) discuss the results by sharing their initial thoughts and observations (5–7 minutes).
5. Have each group select two areas where they feel the results were the most shocking, and ask them to jot down 3–4 possible root causes of or questions they have about each area (10–15 minutes). Collect responses for future discussion and use.
6. Have each table discuss belief and how it affects the culture and climate of a building.

Leadership teaching point: At the conclusion of the activity, lead a discussion about what the results say about collective efficacy and the beliefs held by staff. Discuss how belief affects the climate and culture (both positively and negatively) for both staff and students. This should serve as a lead-in to a larger discussion about working together to continue to build (or maintain, if the results are positive) the necessary belief to carry on as agents for change in meeting the needs of all students. Use Chapter 4, "Building Efficacy," as a resource to craft talking points.

FIGURE 4.7
I Believe Survey

Using a rating scale of 1 to 10 (with 10 meaning you strongly agree), respond to the following statements:	
I believe that I make a difference in the lives of all students.	1 2 3 4 5 6 7 8 9 10
I believe that we should hold all students to the same level of expectations.	1 2 3 4 5 6 7 8 9 10
I believe that all students want to learn.	1 2 3 4 5 6 7 8 9 10
I believe that students are in charge of their learning.	1 2 3 4 5 6 7 8 9 10
I believe that all students can learn.	1 2 3 4 5 6 7 8 9 10
I believe that some circumstances are too challenging for students to overcome.	1 2 3 4 5 6 7 8 9 10
I believe that my teaching will only go so far without help from the student's home.	1 2 3 4 5 6 7 8 9 10
I believe that I have the support I need from administration to make a difference.	1 2 3 4 5 6 7 8 9 10
I believe that I have the support I need from colleagues to make a difference.	1 2 3 4 5 6 7 8 9 10
I believe that I possess the needed skills to reach students with challenging behaviors.	1 2 3 4 5 6 7 8 9 10
I believe that my colleagues possess the needed skills to reach students with challenging behaviors.	1 2 3 4 5 6 7 8 9 10
I believe administration is effectively addressing students' challenging behaviors.	1 2 3 4 5 6 7 8 9 10

5

Normalizing Action

*"Too often the educational value of doing well
what is done, however little, is overlooked. One thing well
done prepares the mind to do the next thing better.
Not how much, but how well, should be the motto.
One problem thoroughly understood is of more value
than a score poorly mastered."*

—Booker T. Washington

We now come to the final point in the Equity Leadership Framework—normalize action. Common or normalized measures that focus on expanding situational awareness around equity are essential to bolster the day-to-day use of an equity lens. Using an equity lens enables us to sense conditions of inequity in the moment or in the context of daily happenings. Building staff awareness of inequity is one thing; developing their ability to detect inequitable situations during everyday interactions is another.

Let's first consider what we mean by the term *equity lens*. We commonly think it involves being all-inclusive in our mental and physical approach. But let's look at what being "all inclusive" really means. The strength of an equity lens is tied to our introspection. Therefore, to authentically exercise an equity lens, we may need to reprogram our minds. Our ego has a human nature side that is grounded in the belief that our way of thinking is the reality. We need to go to the next level of introspection; that is, we need to tame our self-centered perspective, which is governed by our hidden biases, to consider other points of view and conditions of marginalization.

This is more easily said than done. Our biographies and backgrounds have built a solid foundation for how we observe and respond to our environment. Challenging or undoing the years of data points we have used to construct a personal view can be problematic when our history is constantly, and most often unknowingly, playing in the background. Mastering an equity lens requires three gears (inner awareness, situational awareness, and outer awareness) relentlessly grinding to keep our inner ego in check (see Figure 5.1, p. 82).

The function of these gears is paramount to individuals assuming *action-oriented* dispositions (the fifth and highest level of racial consciousness, as discussed in Chapter 3). Beyond supporting staff with these gears, leaders need to keep two agreements front and center to encourage the construction and maintenance of a healthy equity lens.

First, we must remain hyper-focused on isolating race. Because of structural racism and racial bias, race is a multiplier of a host of other conditions. For example, consider educating students who face conditions of poverty. Although poverty certainly negatively affects all race groups, the burden of this condition presents a different level of challenge for those who must also navigate the complexities of racism. Consequently, we cannot effectively address poverty *without isolating race* to understand the intricacies of its effect. Failing to do so breeds inequality.

Second, we must rely on reflection to ensure normalized action around equity. In other words, leaders must shift the tide by taking actions that require staff to become "conscious of craft" (Green, 1985, p. 4). This means that they have acquired the capacity for self-governance by possessing a deep understanding of when they have done something well, when they could have done things better, and when certain actions are simply unacceptable (Green, 1985).

Taking daily action to increase situational awareness is essential to transforming the ecosystem. There are two approaches for doing so: one is through data, and the other is through instructional practice. When used deliberately, data can transform the culture because they can disrupt comfortable routines (Schmoker, 1996). A focus on pedagogical practice builds an understanding of which educational experiences prevent and which ones promote equitable learning outcomes. Let's look at both in more depth.

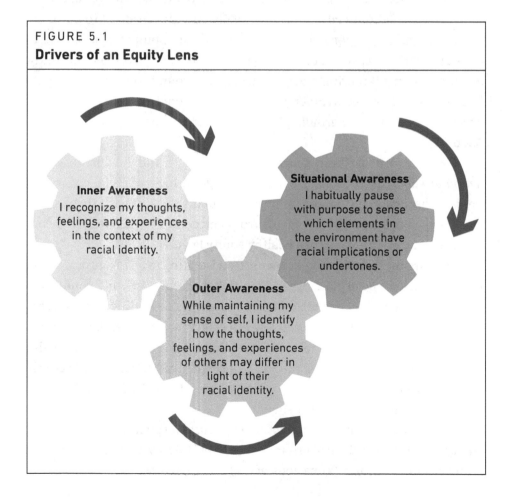

FIGURE 5.1
Drivers of an Equity Lens

Inner Awareness
I recognize my thoughts, feelings, and experiences in the context of my racial identity.

Situational Awareness
I habitually pause with purpose to sense which elements in the environment have racial implications or undertones.

Outer Awareness
While maintaining my sense of self, I identify how the thoughts, feelings, and experiences of others may differ in light of their racial identity.

Using Data for Disruption

In Chapter 3, we talked about the need for creating constructive discomfort and about how transformative change around equity happens by forming a comfortably uncomfortable culture. Using data to create systemic disruption will test a culture's ability to embrace that discomfort.

For data to effectively lead a culture to liberation, leaders must be able to count on strong relationships within the system. As Shane Safir (2017) points out, relationships are currency in schools; relational capital is like a big savings account of trust and goodwill. Cultures that have established a higher level of trust and goodwill will bounce back more readily from difficult conversations. And if schools are having the right conversations, there will be struggle. In the words of Frederick Douglass, "If there is no struggle, there is no progress."

Schools working to achieve a culture of equity must rely on data to establish a clear picture of the current reality, help stakeholders better understand what measures are affecting which individuals and why, and provide regular feedback that enables appropriate course corrections. Although schools working toward continuous improvement are accustomed to reviewing data, getting stakeholders to let down their guard to truly invest in the process can pose quite a challenge.

Lori, a fourth-year secondary school principal, recalls her staff's reactions to using data in this way. Here are some of their concerns:

- "There's too much data to look at, which makes it confusing."
- "All staff members should not see data that point to the weaknesses of individual teachers."
- "Data are not always dependable because they don't account for uncontrollable factors."
- "Students are more than just data points."
- "We've looked at the data. Now what? We don't have time to implement all these changes."

Many school leaders I've talked with share a common experience of meeting opposition once staff perceive that a new data focus will disrupt comfortable routines. In addition to the natural discomfort that may arise when reviewing data, there's also the uneasiness individuals may feel when talking about race. Figure 5.2 shows some of the similarities in the reactions people experience when they engage in these pursuits.

FIGURE 5.2

The Discomfort Factor: Reviewing Data and Talking About Race

Factor	Reviewing Data	Talking About Race
Exhaustion	Because of the time and thinking involved, the process of deeply examining data can be overwhelming.	Because of the time and mental processing involved, some will wonder how long these types of conversations must go on.
Vulnerability	The process can be highly emotional because it exposes who we are.	These conversations can expose a side of reality that we're not used to experiencing or seeing.
Frustration	The process can cause feelings of guilt and shame.	These conversations can bring us into conflict with ourselves, causing feelings of guilt and shame.
Defensiveness	The process can cause us to defend or protect our character.	These conversations can cause us to defend or protect our privilege.
Second-guessing	The process can cause stress because it can call into question things we have done.	These conversations can cause stress because they can call into question things we have been taught or socialized to believe.
Anxiety	The process can make us uneasy because we sense at the end there will be additional work involved.	These conversations can make us uneasy because we sense that we're being asked to do more (by giving up our privilege or comfort).
Shifting attention or blame	The process can cause us to point to areas that shift the conversation to other topics of perceived importance.	These conversations can cause us to point to areas that move the conversation to other topics of perceived importance.

To soften the blow, some leaders might communicate the idea that "we're doing the best we can," whereas others might share only the "right" data to ensure no one gets called out or develops emotional scars. All such approaches compromise the sense of urgency and the need for change that the data are, in fact, revealing.

Leaders can build coherence around data in the following ways to allow for disruption.

Create a Clear Path

For data to effectively interfere with deep-rooted institutional practices, stakeholders must collectively commit to seek out problems, take ownership of shortcomings, and implement accountability measures that hold a high standard for change. Staff need to trust the process.

Recognizing her staff's negative reactions to using data in this way, Principal Lori infused the following core beliefs in the school culture:

- **This is not a crime investigation.** Looking at data is never about shaming others or creating a sense of guilt.
- **Examining data is like looking at ourselves in the mirror.** We're not always going to be comfortable with what we see, but data reveal what is there.
- **Examining data is an opportunity and a necessity for growth.** It's a chance to get to know ourselves better, and getting to know ourselves better is never a bad thing.
- **Data serve as a directional road sign.** Data are both an affirmation and a caution signal. They help us uncover our blind spots and keep us on our desired path.
- **Let's focus on our circle of influence.** This is an opportunity to address the things we *can* control.

As Lori noted about her leadership approach,

If I wanted teachers to thrive in using data and not feel threatened, my actions had to communicate that they could trust the process and rely on my support. I had to be consistent in showing alignment with my beliefs and actions and cognizant of which core beliefs were a struggle for staff so I could promptly provide support. I also needed to collaborate consistently, working intently beside staff to prevent the perception of a top-down approach to change.

If data are going to effectively disrupt the system, staff must feel comfortable with the intentions of their school leader. If they perceive that the leader's objective in using data is positive, their increased trust will allow for greater vulnerability and accountability.

Get to the Fundamental Truth, and Start Anew

In a one-on-one TED interview with Chris Anderson in 2013, Elon Musk explained the notion of *first principles thinking* in this way: "What I mean by that is boil things down to their fundamental truths and reason up from there, as opposed to reasoning by analogy" (Xoofish, 2013). Let's look at this idea in the context of using data for disruption. Schools commonly respond to data by improving on current practices or taking what other schools are doing and making it their own. A problem that easily arises with this approach is that improvement remains at the surface level while issues still lurk at the core. True disruption is about tearing down widely held practices, beliefs, and assumptions that perpetuate culturally oppressive states and starting anew. This means first taking time to understand the nature of the problem and then building from there.

Seek Out the Untold Narrative

Data can uncover a story. Disproportionate gaps and other negative results should provoke a quest for learning more about those who are disenfranchised. That means that the data must elicit and heavily rely on the voices of the oppressed. To discover root causes, we must not only seek out the experiences and stories of the oppressed but also be able to truly hear them. The path to disruption involves searching for and uncovering the untold narrative and exercising authentic listening to identify and address needs.

Don't Wait for Data to Come to You

Although looking at annual data serves a purpose, be intentional in both collecting and monitoring data that provide routine feedback on day-to-day efforts to achieve equity. More frequent opportunities to view data allow for greater appreciation of the role of data, heightened awareness of individual and collective impact, and a shared sense of accountability. To help schools disrupt patterns of marginalization among race groups, I offer the following five-step Equity Lens Analysis approach to examining data. (In the

Appendix, the downloadable Tool C—the Planning Form for Equity Action Strategy Development—can help you organize your thoughts on the matter.)

1. **Gather.** Determine the data you would like to review. Consider reviewing multiple data sources (attendance and course enrollment data, behavior/suspension data, extracurricular activity data, climate surveys, common assessments, grading, and so on) to gain an array of perspectives. *Guiding questions:*
   —What data should we organize and review?
   —Will the data we have identified provide enough perspective?
   —Do we need both quantitative and qualitative data?

2. **Gauge.** Look for any observable disparities within the data. Remember to look beyond growth. Although you may find that trend data for students of color indicate growth rates similar to the growth rates of their nonminority peers, don't assume that overall gaps are closing. In many instances, students of color must outperform their counterparts for gaps to narrow. *Guiding questions:*
   —What are the overall trends by race as well as by cohorts of students?
   —Are students of color growing similarly to their nonminority peers?
   —Do various programs show disproportionality in representation?
   —Do our surveys indicate disproportionate experiences?
   —Do various groups of students show similar indicators of school connectedness (for example, in terms of attendance, behavior, student engagement, extracurricular activities, and climate surveys)?

3. **Grapple.** Wrestle with your data to confront factors that contribute to the results you're finding. *Guiding questions:*
   —How are these data affecting teaching and learning?
   —What is the story behind the data? (If, on the basis of our data, we had to publicly share the experience of students of color, what would we say?)
   —If our data reveal disparities, what specific actions perpetuate those disparities?
   —Do the patterns or trends in our data indicate that specific grade levels, classrooms, or parts of the building are more heavily affected than others?
   —Do any of our data speak to positional freedom or hidden bias? How so?

4. **Glean.** Identify who can provide an additional voice to expand on the results you're finding. How will you elicit and learn from the voices that are missing from the table? This will be an essential step when building coherence and sustaining momentum toward growth and change. *Guiding questions:*
   —Whom do we need to hear from, based on the data?
   —How will we engage with those missing from the table to honor their voices?
   —What did we learn from the voices we solicited?
   —How do their stories confirm or contradict our beliefs and perceptions?
   —How will we show that we have truly heard the stories or experiences they shared?
   —How will we keep them engaged? How will we follow up with them?

5. **Game plan.** Strategize a purposeful approach to addressing the data. Lay a path with reasonable timelines and actionable measures of accountability. *Guiding questions:*
   —What are our biggest challenges with equity and race?
   —What barriers do we need to remove?
   —What strategy do we need in place to provide better support in identified areas?
   —How do we strengthen what we know is working?
   —What would a newly designed strategy or policy look like from a multicultural perspective?
   —How will we communicate our plan and monitor progress?
   —How will we know we have reached our goals?

The Equity Lens Analysis approach will not only strengthen the level of consciousness among staff about race but also result in the following benefits:

- It will identify culturally oppressive conditions and solution-based outcomes.
- It will enable staff to learn from key stakeholders.
- It will define the fundamental beliefs and practices that reinforce and are at the root of systemic conditions.

- It will tear down strategies and practices that promote disparities, thus allowing for the removal of barriers with racial implications.
- It will promote the adoption of strategies with a multicultural perspective.

LEADERSHIP TIP

Here are some additional norms and guiding questions to support a deeper conversation when using the Equity Lens Analysis approach. This will come in handy as you *gauge* and *grapple* with your data:

- **Naming brings power.** If you see apparent racial disparities or indications of bias in your data, call them out. This will be uncomfortable at first, but this is the kryptonite to battling systemic racism.
- **Unpack thoughts and feelings.** Having acknowledged the presence of racial bias, you can look closer to consider its sources and ramifications. *Guiding questions:*
  - Why are we bothered by calling out this data as an indication of racism, discrimination, and so on?
  - What contributes to the situation we have identified? Who is advantaged by it, and in what ways? What are the hidden positional freedoms? Is this stereotypical? If so, how?
  - What rules or structures are creating disparity or disadvantage?
- **Choose a different seat.** Force yourself to see things from another's perspective. Although we cannot fully know another's thoughts or experiences, part of disruption is seeking to understand. This process will be challenging, and some will wish to skip it entirely, but push through it anyway. *Guiding questions:*
  - What does this information say about the experience of _____ (the disparaged group)?
  - How might they interpret this information or see it differently?
  - What parts of their story are we missing?
- **Challenge the system.** Name and examine the building rules, policies, or practices that are implicated in the data. *Guiding questions:*
  - How is this (rule, policy, or practice) creating an advantage/ disadvantage?
  - Who is it creating an advantage/disadvantage for?

- **Challenge yourselves.** Name and challenge stereotypes or conditions of racism that are being perpetuated. *Guiding questions:*
  —How have we contributed to the disparities or conditions of racism revealed in these data?
  —How are we helping to create the advantage/disadvantage that our data show?
  —How does our cultural narrative (biographies and backgrounds) inadvertently affect the data through our interactions or decisions?
- **Master the call.** Instead of calling one another out when deficit discourse begins to surface, adults should *call one another in*. The following are some tips to help guide staff around a practice of calling in:
  —When an individual shares deficit words or thoughts, always address them from a place of positive assumption and care.
  —Explain your concern with the deficit comment by repeating what you heard and the message you believe it communicates. For example, "I would like to call in something I just heard you mention. When you said _____, here is what I heard: _____. Can we talk about what you mean?"
  —Pay attention to your delivery when calling someone in. Be sure to interact with a genuine desire to understand and learn through active listening. Calling someone in is not about winning anyone over with our point; however, it *is* about having enough respect for someone to engage in this type of conversation.

In using the Equity Lens Analysis approach, be sure to consider non-traditional data points, such as budgeting and hiring practices. As for the former, funding that supports the goal of equity is crucial. As for the latter, research has shown that teachers of color are integral not only to the learning experiences of students of color but also to those of all students (National Center for Education Statistics, 2020).

Using Pedagogical Practices to Enhance Equity

In addition to using data for disruption in the pursuit of equity, leaders can also look at the teaching practices taking place in their buildings. Before diving into specific strategies and methods, I want to first clarify a crucial point: I believe that most teachers are well intentioned and believe in their charge to educate effectively. But because race is a social construct that works for the benefit of some and to the detriment of others, symptoms of systemic racial segregation easily surface in the classroom unbeknownst to teachers.

Zaretta Hammond (2015) shares the following:

> A critical first step for teachers is to understand how their cultural values shape their expectations in the classroom—from how they expect children to behave socially, take turns during discussion, or even pass out classroom materials. A student's different way of being or doing can be perceived as a deviation from the norm and therefore problematic if we don't recognize that it is just different. (pp. 55–56)

Leaders must help teachers strengthen their ability to step outside themselves. This involves looking for practices and strategies that are responsive to the various cultures represented in the classroom or that are mindful of equity. As Baruti Kafele (2021) notes, "If a classroom is going to be a truly equity-based environment, it is going to require an equity mindset teacher" (p. 17).

For teachers to be influential allies for students of color, they need to focus on three areas:

- **Inspired instruction.** *Are educators conveying joy and excitement for the teaching material during instruction?* Inspired instruction creates real-world connections with students and fosters intrinsic motivation because it values students as learners.
- **Positive pursuance.** *Are educators relentlessly seeking to obtain unbiased outcomes in learning?* Here, teachers guard against assumptions about underserved students as learners that deny opportunities that may stretch student thinking. Teachers don't allow students to opt out, and they hold high expectations for all students regardless of circumstance. They spend less time lecturing, and they don't prematurely rescue students before the students engage in critical thinking. In addition, they may plan purposeful opportunities for students of color to make mistakes to assist them in becoming resilient learners. This is in no way struggle for the sake of struggle. Rather, it's about opportunities for diverse learners to endure productive failure and exert mental sweat. Finally, positive pursuance assumes that educators believe that they can and do make a difference. Teachers set achievement goals and

then gradually release the responsibility of learning to the students to foster independent learners.

- **The unseen curriculum.** *Are educators aware of the unseen curriculum?* Educators need to understand the norms, values, and beliefs that subconsciously play out in the classroom. That entails paying attention to established conditions and teacher actions that might contribute to disengagement in the classroom for students of color. Does the unseen curriculum permit students of color to see and be themselves? Does instruction embrace uniqueness, avoid perpetuating stereotypes, and communicate a high expectancy that all students will become competent, independent learners?

Because Black students depend on educator support to counter the myths of inferiority (Delpit, 2012), having teachers who are competent in connecting with diverse students is crucial to their pursuit of learning. To quote Delpit (1995), in thinking about instructional practice,

> the key... is not the kind of instruction but the attitude underlying it. When teachers do not understand the potential of the students they teach, they will under teach them no matter what the methodology. (p. 175)

LEADERSHIP TIP

Along with the three conditions noted—inspired instruction, positive pursuance, and the unseen curriculum—the following are additional examples of culturally responsive practices that leaders should support and look for:

- **Relating to student experiences.** Diverse students see themselves and experience a sense of belonging when teachers celebrate and listen to their various stories and provide opportunities to explore other cultures.
- **Supporting student identity.** Because diverse students commonly contend with intersecting identities (school, home, peers, and so on), it's vital to get to know them and embrace who they are. The more teachers understand their students, the greater their ability to strengthen student identity through encouragement and affirmation.
- **Strengthening critical thinking.** To ignite learning, we must approach culturally diverse students with purposeful strategies that expand their

ability to think critically. Teachers must push past student compliance by asking higher-level questions that probe the student's depth of knowledge and advance learning.

- **Promoting socially relevant learning.** Teachers need to make learning socially relevant by providing opportunities for diverse learners to engage purposefully with peers.
- **Holding high expectations**. Higher expectations help diverse learners build resilience to stick with challenges and see themselves as capable learners.
- **Connecting to prior knowledge.** By recognizing and planning around their prior learning, teachers can help diverse students connect the dots by tapping into their background knowledge.
- **Checking for understanding.** When teachers fail to gauge students' understanding of content during the course of instruction (Schmoker, 2016), they inadvertently fail to nurture thought processes as students seek to make sense of their learning. Equity-minded teachers continually check for understanding to assess student learning and make informed instructional decisions.

The Appendix's Tool D—the Classroom Observation Guide for Culturally Responsive Strategies—can help you help teachers strengthen their practices in this area.

Spotlight on Practice: The Equity Walk

Supporting instructional practice is one of the most crucial functions principals can engage in as they assist teachers in becoming educational equity allies. One effective approach is the equity walk. Equity walks are a targeted way for leadership teams and schools to collect data focused on equity with the intent of facilitating awareness and action through conversations. Following are some tips for creating effective equity walks.

Set a Clear Purpose

Equity walks involve leaders and coaches going into classrooms to determine the status of equity across the building. Leaders should embrace this process as a way of determining if they are effectively supporting staff, as opposed to documenting what staff members are doing wrong. In other words, teachers must understand that this process is not for evaluative purposes.

Leaders or coaches can visit classrooms in pairs or individually, although going in pairs may allow coverage of a larger area in a classroom. Equity walks must include reflective coaching conversations that help teachers become aware of practices that make cultural connections and that encourage them to use growth mindset language in the classroom.

Leaders and coaches can use the Equity Environment Scan shown in Figure 5.3 to focus equity walks. The tool provides a scale for measuring patterns of equity in three areas: instruction, emotional resilience, and the environment. Observers don't need to collect all this information at once; they can select focus areas for each walk and collect the pertinent data that way. The primary purpose of this instrument is to enable leaders to calibrate themselves around conditions supporting equity, use the data to have meaningful coaching conversations, and provide better instructional leadership support to staff. When using this tool, you don't need to wait in a classroom until the "magic" happens, but it is important to remain long enough to get a good sense of what's taking place there. Once you have obtained the evidence, use the Guide to Culturally Responsive Strategy Patterns (Tool E in the Appendix; see p. 120) to assess the degree of equity in that classroom.

You can form larger equity teams of leaders, coaches, and teachers to view the results of data and create strategies around themes. Transparency is important here. Keep in mind that to support a culture of trust, leaders need to give all staff members the opportunity to reflect on collective data from the equity walks. Be sure to give staff access to both Figure 5.3's Equity Environment Scan and the Classroom Observation Guide for Culturally Responsive Strategies (Tool D in the Appendix; see p. 119). These powerful mechanisms can help individuals grow through self-reflection. In addition, the conversation norms and activities provided in this book should help you establish a routine of collaborative conversation and feedback around race and equity that support peer coaching discussions.

Individuals can also self-coach using these tools. Teachers can capture one of their lessons on video, then observe the lesson closely to see where they fall on the Equity Environment Scan. Over time, coaches could use these reflection sheets as part of a conversation with teachers to check on their progress in this area.

FIGURE 5.3
Equity Environment Scan

Instructional Impact

The overall teaching style communicates rigor.

Low Pattern   Some Pattern   High Pattern

Observation Evidence:

Learning goals communicate a higher standard of learning (beyond basic application).

Low Pattern   Some Pattern   High Pattern

Observation Evidence:

Students are clear about their learning.

Low Pattern   Some Pattern   High Pattern

Observation Evidence:

All learners are engaged in good fit activities.

Low Pattern   Some Pattern   High Pattern

Observation Evidence:

All learners are asked to respond to higher-level questions.

Low Pattern   Some Pattern   High Pattern

Observation Evidence:

(continued)

FIGURE 5.3—(*continued*)
Equity Environment Scan

Emotional Resilience

Students are expected to participate/engage in learning. (Who is opting out?)

Low Pattern   Some Pattern   High Pattern

Supporting Evidence:

Students are given time to process and think.

Low Pattern   Some Pattern   High Pattern

Supporting Evidence:

Student thinking is affirmed or nurtured as the students seek solutions.

Low Pattern   Some Pattern   High Pattern

Supporting Evidence:

Students receive immediate/timely feedback.

Low Pattern   Some Pattern   High Pattern

Supporting Evidence:

Lower-ability students receive specific feedback.

Low Pattern   Some Pattern   High Pattern

Supporting Evidence:

Learning Environment

The classroom is strategically arranged to promote a sense of equity.

Low Pattern   Some Pattern   High Pattern

Supporting Evidence:

Students can see themselves in the learning environment (in books, materials, etc.).

Low Pattern   Some Pattern   High Pattern

Supporting Evidence:

Behavior expectations are consistently applied and culturally responsive to learners.

Low Pattern   Some Pattern   High Pattern

Supporting Evidence:

All students feel safe to ask questions and explore their knowledge.

Low Pattern   Some Pattern   High Pattern

Supporting Evidence:

The room promotes and showcases a higher standard of academic learning.

Low Pattern   Some Pattern   High Pattern

Supporting Evidence:

Set a Schedule

Equity walks should not be a surprise visit. Leaders and coaches should give staff advance notice and be purposeful in visiting classrooms. Staff should feel supported during this process. Make sure you clarify that it's not about fixing teachers; rather, it's about enhancing leadership's understanding of the state of equity in their buildings. Observers should stay long enough in the classroom to truly understand what the teachers are doing and what challenges they face. Make equity walks a part of your building routine. Set a schedule, communicate in advance, and commit to keeping that schedule.

Strategize for Effective Coaching

Leaders should use the data collected during equity walks to promote quality conversations through coaching. Because we don't want this process to feel evaluative, the question for leaders becomes how to effectively communicate and build support around the conclusions found in the data.

Examine the following coaching conversation between a principal and his teacher, Ms. Jones. The teacher had a goal of establishing a stronger relationship with two of her most defiant students, who happen to be students of color:

Principal: It was great to be in your classroom today to watch you working with students during math. As always, I'd like to start by hearing your thoughts on the lesson.

Ms. Jones: Well... overall, I felt like the instructional part of the lesson went well for most students. However, I'm sure you noticed Jaxon and Kenneth made the lesson "interesting." I'm doing everything I can, but their behavior really impedes their ability to connect to the concepts. And it negatively affects everyone sitting around them too.

Principal: I noticed you used some of the culturally relevant engagement strategies we've been practicing schoolwide. It was great seeing this take place in your classroom. So I know you've been working on your goal of building a stronger relationship with both Jaxon and Kenneth. What specific strategies have you tried, and what difference have they made?

Ms. Jones: I have tried some new strategies. I've tried to better understand the cultural challenges that Jaxon and Kenneth face. Still, I'm not sure their behavior has anything to do with race. We've done a lot of talking about cultural differences, but there are so many other ways to look at what is happening with these students, and I'm not convinced race is the right one.

Principal: I agree that there are a lot of things that shape our students and their behavior, and race should not be the sole focus. But to go along with our previous conversations, to understand how you can have a positive influence on each student, we need to continue to reflect on your values, beliefs, and practices while considering how Jaxon and Kenneth's behavior may be shaped by the cultural experiences they perceive.

Ms. Jones: It might help if you can give me an example of something you saw during my lesson when I was not considering Jaxon or Kenneth.

Principal: Sure, let's look at some of the evidence I found while focusing on the Emotional Resilience Scale [see Tool E in the Appendix]. It's under the section "Students are expected to participate and engage in learning" (who is opting out). I noticed there were a couple of times you attempted to pull Jaxon and Kenneth into the discussion, but when they didn't engage, you moved on to other students. Then they began to act out further. I'd be interested in hearing your thoughts about why you decided to move on and the possible cultural message that might inadvertently send. And how might this affect your goal of building a stronger relationship with each student?

The key point for leaders to remember in regularly collecting and discussing classroom data is that it's all about how the process makes staff feel. As we can see with Ms. Jones, she still needs convincing to fully commit to focusing on equity by keeping an eye on race. The principal needs to remain thoughtful in this conversation. Otherwise, it risks going down the path of "transference." In this scenario, that means allowing Ms. Jones to deflect her issues with race, turning the focus of conversation onto more digestible areas of concern.

In Figure 5.4, you'll find a tool designed to build the capacity of leaders and coaches to effectively approach coaching conversations focused on data collected during equity walks (a template for this "REFLECT" planning

FIGURE 5.4
Coaching for Equity Action Plan: REFLECT

Rationalize. *What is the purpose of providing this feedback?* Before engaging in a coaching conversation, think through what you want to communicate and why:
- What equitable practices are working well?
- What behavior changes will better support inclusiveness for all learners?
- What aspects of equity will I focus on in providing my feedback?
- What specific words will I use in referencing equitable and inequitable behaviors?

Empathize. *How will I show compassion regarding how the person might feel while receiving this feedback?* Planning how you will communicate a sense of compassion and collaboration will be beneficial in establishing the individual's trust and motivation to act on received feedback:
- What actions and words will I use to communicate that we're learning together?
- What parts of my feedback may cause discomfort?
- What will I do or say when I notice discomfort?
- How will I monitor my listening to stay actively engaged in hearing and understanding the individual's point of view?

Focus. *How will I "stay curious"?* Guard against dominating the conversation, making personal judgments, and asking questions that may seem accusatory:
- How will I monitor myself to ensure that I'm not dominating the conversation with personal views and opinions?
- How will I guard against making personal judgments?
- How will I remain mindful of asking questions that are not accusatory?

Learn. *How can I be helpful?* Be mindful of the setting where the conversation takes place, how you position yourself, and the tone of the conversation. Contemplate how you might model active listening:
- How will I provide a safe space for individuals to reflect on their ability to leverage equitable practices during the lesson?
- How will I model listening to select key areas or themes necessary to push their practices forward through reflective questioning?

Engage. *How can I communicate in the most honest and accurate way?* Think through what questions might promote the individual's deep thinking and future self-monitoring of their practice. Truthfully communicate observations without embellishing them:
- What questions can I ask that promote thinking about desired behaviors?
- How will I keep the conversation collaborative and focused on helping the person self-monitor their effect on learning outcomes?
- What is the best way to speak my truth honestly and accurately regarding what went well and where practices can improve? *Don't embellish when it's your time to speak.*

Check. *Is joint understanding in place?* Think through how you might check in with individuals to ensure they understand the ramifications their actions have on student learning outcomes:
- How will I circle back to ensure there's a joint understanding of a path forward?
- How will I know the individual understands the ramifications of desired or undesired actions on unbiased outcomes in learning?

Target. *What are the important takeaways? When will there be a follow-up?* Clarify when you will follow up with the individual and how you will affirm next steps or goals at the end of the conversation:
- If the person struggles with defining next steps, what next steps might I identify?
- Given what I observed or the nature of the classroom, when would be an appropriate time to follow up?
- How will I clearly affirm expectations or goals for the follow-up conversation?

approach is available in the Appendix; see Tool F, p. 126). It's designed to help leaders think through how to maintain a disposition that communicates support during challenging feedback conversations. Here are a few essential points to support transformational change in such discussions:

- **The conversation is not all about race, but race certainly matters.** Don't lose the context of race as you move through the conversation.
- **Avoid false positive feedback.** You can't afford to ignore observed conditions, beliefs, actions, or instructional moves that marginalize students and, instead, simply focus on the positive. This clouds current realities, creates a false narrative, and permits and promotes inequity.
- **Speak truth (with humanity).** Commit to telling individuals what they need to hear, but think through how you can do it with care.

LEADERSHIP TIP

Be sure to approach these coaching conversations through your equity lens. Understand your societal position or the cultural context you're bringing to the discussion, and be aware of the cultural perspective of the individual you're coaching. Here are some suggestions:

- **Know the power you hold.** Your title is not the only thing bringing power to the conversation. In fact, it may create some hesitancy in others when they're deciding whether to be open with you. The color of your skin can also bring power. For example, suppose you're a leader from a dominant cultural group. In that case, teachers of color are contending with both your title and your overshadowing cultural narrative, which they know will make it even harder for you to understand where they're coming from if they decide to be open. On the other hand, leaders of color may have to contend with deficit ideologies when they engage in such conversations.
- **Channel your inner voice.** Because your narrative holds power (good, bad, or indifferent), try to maintain situational awareness of how the individual you're speaking with is perceiving your words and body language. Pay attention to your ego, which may try to place others in a box centered around your morals, your values, and your beliefs.
- **Avoid the snare of assumption.** Be careful not to make assumptions about others' personal experiences, values, or beliefs. Also, don't assume that everyone can always be themselves during the conversation. For

example, people of color may experience a polarity between wanting to be their authentic selves and not wanting to affirm racial stereotypes.

- **Be on a quest.** Envision your mind as a blank canvas during the conversation. Be an active listener on a quest to learn as much as you can about another's experiences. Don't seek to impose your narrative; engage in a way that aims to form a shared narrative around given situations. You will need to deeply listen to connect to another's reality and relate it to what you observed.

Making the Most of Time

It's crucial to take an approach to leadership that builds the habits of both data-informed action *and* adult reflection on instructional practice. Investing in each area, as part of individual teacher goal setting, classroom observation and discussion, summative evaluation discussion, peer observations/ instructional rounds, or collaborative grade-level discussion, will enhance your staff's daily equity lens.

Yes, sparking a culture that honors all students will require devoting the appropriate amount of time and effort to each process, but the investment is well worth it.

Next Steps for Leaders: Become a Lead Learner

Robinson and colleagues (2008) found that the most significant factor influencing the effect that school principals have on student learning is the level at which the principal learns with staff to move improvement efforts forward. As you are leading the way through data and coaching support, don't neglect your obligation to this crucial role. When you learn with staff, you strengthen relationships, bring consistency to adult action, increase a sense of care and accountability, and effectively monitor the effect of systemic conditions. In other words, sustainability depends on your ability to guide the way as a lead learner.

Ask yourself...

- Are we effectively leveraging data to disrupt inequitable practices within our environment?
- How are we supporting equity through teachers' instructional practice?
- How can we better leverage coaching conversations to strengthen the equity lens of staff?

6

Acquiring Hope

"Change does not roll in on the wheels of inevitability,
but comes through continuous struggle."

—Martin Luther King Jr.

I began this book by telling the story of a principal named Terry and how, after five years of implementing strategies to achieve equity, he and his staff were still getting results that didn't reflect the effort they were putting in. We then discussed the notion of *coherence* and the need for leaders to build a deep-rooted organizational understanding of why equity is paramount and how to genuinely form it. As we looked at how to support a collective awareness of equity, we came to the Equity Leadership Framework.

Here's what leaders need to focus on in each component of this ongoing cycle:

- **Defining and clarifying equity.** Take a systematic approach to build consensus around a common definition and vision of equity. This is the foundation upon which all things will flow. Everyone needs to be on the same page in understanding what equity means and why the work is so crucial for the other framework components to optimally function.
- **Creating discomfort.** Create a new normal where adults get *comfortably uncomfortable.* That means having a culture where individuals challenge racial inequities, deficit ideologies, and ultimately the status quo through intentional dialogue conscious of race.
- **Building efficacy.** Support the development of higher levels of individual and shared efficacy. Monitoring adult beliefs will be crucial to ensuring that staff members make the appropriate efforts and commit to change.
- **Normalizing action.** Ensure that staff are routinely using an equity lens in the areas of data and instruction. Fostering the proper mindsets to disrupt the hidden conditions of racism will require intentionality in each area for consistent and sustained success over time.

For equity work to succeed, the core of the framework—leadership—must be highly functional. Knowing that the road ahead will come with its fair share of second-guessing, uneasiness, opposition, and setbacks, let's conclude this book with a reminder of the importance of your role in this work. Without strong leadership, your school or district will come to a standstill in action when resilience is tested. Remember, consistency in execution requires *focus, competence,* and *passion* from leadership.

The Need for Focus

Equity fatigue has a way of setting in when you're deeply engaged in this work. Some will grow weary as a result of all the attention and time they're devoting to equity. You can strengthen resilience by continually revisiting the importance of equity; remember, connecting to a sense of purpose engenders rejuvenation.

However, a caveat here: don't become so driven that the work is more about *doing equity* than truly undertaking the *cause* of equity. When leaders engage in "doing equity," they go through the motions, as if working through a checklist, or seek outside experts to take over the work. But no one-size-fits-all approach will work, and external support can only take you so far. This is not to say that the school shouldn't look to outsiders for support. However, there can be a tendency to lay idle, waiting until the "savior" returns to deliver the next professional development session on the topic.

Undertaking the cause of equity is about leaders who keep their minds on the mission, diligently remain at the forefront, and engage stakeholders as critical partners in the work. You may bring others in for support, but in the end, it's your leadership that will most influence the level of equity your staff achieves.

The Need for Competence

Transformational change in the environment is largely a social process. Your ability to establish systemic structures and practices that build constructive *shared experiences* is essential to the mission.

Innately, we are built for relationships, and whether we like it or not, experiences are the *glue* that bonds us together. Just think about it. Even negative experiences with people in our lives have a way of following us and connecting us to them, sometimes for our entire lives. When a leader is skilled in establishing conditions that foster appropriate adult connections, it alters the environment through the strengthened bond and commitment among its people. This is not to say that the experiences are smooth and without bumps. However, it does imply that a skillful leader can move those within the culture down a path to better both themselves and the world around them.

The Need for Passion

Be passionate about the people who are working with you. Commit your-self to understanding their perspective on what's happening in your school. Search within and outside your inner circles to piece together the current reality from a variety of angles. If tension exists in your environment, seek out the voices of those who have not yet been heard.

When faced with challenges, we can only choose paths or arrive at solutions that are informed by our knowledge. A lack of knowledge or experience threatens our ability to lead and respond effectively. Being a highly capable leader means being able to speak to the heart, soul, and minds of those who must join you to achieve change.

Where Hope Is Lost

There's no easy path to transformative change. Even if you use the Equity Leadership Framework and other ideas covered in this book, the work will remain complex. Kegan and Lahey (2009) remind us of how resistant people can be to change by sharing that even after cardiac patients were told they would literally die if they didn't change their diet, take up exercise, or quit smoking, only one in seven were able to do so.

We tend to resist new ways of doing things that we perceive pose a threat to our comfort, safety, and security. When school staff grasp the kinds of changes needed to champion equity, they may have an aversion to losing a sense of normalcy, and you may have difficulty convincing them of the need to do this work. But it's not just a matter of getting people to recognize systemic racism; it's also about bringing them to a willingness to adopt the practices needed to negate conditions founded in racism. When facing a lift of this magnitude, the time and patience it will require may test your optimism.

The world of education may have changed in the wake of COVID-19, but the pandemic of racism has been a factor within it for much longer and remains strong. Despite efforts to raise students' academic trajectory through various "vaccination" efforts over the years, systemic racism is still affecting our most vulnerable population—students of color. Doors to certain opportunities remain disproportionally locked against these young people, and their achievement lags. Too many educators have yet to commit to the kind of actions necessary to advance equity, and many seem reluctant, if not unwilling, to endure the uneasiness this process is sure to bring about. The challenges are real, and the roadblocks are daunting. Even though you believe in the cause of equity, it's easy to lose hope.

Where Hope Is Found

One evening during this past winter break, I experienced a life-defining moment while spending time with my youngest son, Zevin. We were playing his favorite video game, and what I thought would be a quick game of virtual hoops turned into a five-hour-long bout because of my determination to win even one game. During the final contest, I was trailing by 20 points in the third quarter when I finally realized it was time to give up for the night. Accepting this reality, I humbly commented, "Dad is calling it quits as soon as we finish this game."

But then something started to click. It was as though all the hours I'd spent on this video game suddenly began to pay off. Thanks to the late-game heroics of Steph Curry of the Golden State Warriors, I pulled off a miraculous comeback victory. Shortly after, as my wife and I were preparing for bed, Zevin walked into our bedroom. He hugged me, looked me in the eye, and shared the most profound words I have ever heard come out of a 10-year-old's mouth: "Dad, you know how I knew you were going to win that last game? Because where all hope is lost, that's where hope is found."

Where all hope is lost, that's where hope is found. These words gave me a moment of extreme clarity because they apply to all circumstances in life. What brings hope to this work of equity is effective leadership. In *The Answer Is in the Room: How Effective Schools Scale Up Student Success,* Alan Blankstein (2011) reminds us that the most valuable resource we have is "focused commitment over time" (p. 42) and that we must have faith that the answer is "in the room." As a leader, when you are in the room, hope *can* be found—in you. Leadership matters, and you must believe that you are the X-factor in creating transformational change within your school.

This book opened with an assessment that sought to help you gauge how comfortable you were in leading your staff to address conditions of inequality and racism in your school or district. Now that we have arrived at the end of our journey together, I would like you to retake that assessment (reprinted as Figure 6.1) so you can see how you have grown.

Your post-assessment result should shore up your confidence as an equity leader, and confidence increases your ability to engage others in this work. Hargreaves and Harris (2015) argue that "the impact of effective leaders is especially important when schools operate in challenging circumstances" (p. 28). And there is no more challenging circumstance than eradicating conditions of racism to achieve equity.

Embracing setbacks is an essential part of this journey; although we try to avoid them, they can tell us what does and doesn't work. Most important, understand that nothing gets done without engaging leadership. Engaging

FIGURE 6.1
Leading for Equity: A Post-Assessment

I am comfortable having conversations about conditions of inequality or racism.	☐ Strongly Disagree ☐ Disagree ☐ Neutral ☐ Agree ☐ Strongly Agree
I am comfortable taking the lead in guiding others through conversations that seek to build their awareness around conditions of inequality or racism.	☐ Strongly Disagree ☐ Disagree ☐ Neutral ☐ Agree ☐ Strongly Agree
I am comfortable delivering truthful coaching and feed-back to support others in identifying and addressing instructional practices that are culturally unresponsive.	☐ Strongly Disagree ☐ Disagree ☐ Neutral ☐ Agree ☐ Strongly Agree
I am comfortable with my ability to help others gain the skills necessary to effectively advocate for equity when seeing daily circumstances associated with racial overtones.	☐ Strongly Disagree ☐ Disagree ☐ Neutral ☐ Agree ☐ Strongly Agree
I am comfortable leading others in using data to disrupt racial inequities in my building or district and to establish sound strategies for improvement.	☐ Strongly Disagree ☐ Disagree ☐ Neutral ☐ Agree ☐ Strongly Agree
I am comfortable with my ability to self-reflect regularly to uncover any hidden biases and stereotypes I may possess.	☐ Strongly Disagree ☐ Disagree ☐ Neutral ☐ Agree ☐ Strongly Agree
I am comfortable with my level of understanding around what signifies equity to effectively guide others within my school or district environment in understanding.	☐ Strongly Disagree ☐ Disagree ☐ Neutral ☐ Agree ☐ Strongly Agree
I am comfortable with my ability to provide a sense of value and belief within staff that leads to greater out-comes for marginalized students.	☐ Strongly Disagree ☐ Disagree ☐ Neutral ☐ Agree ☐ Strongly Agree
I am comfortable with my ability to routinely step outside myself to learn how my present reality influenced by race compares with the reality of others.	☐ Strongly Disagree ☐ Disagree ☐ Neutral ☐ Agree ☐ Strongly Agree

leadership inspires and generates an expectation for change, which can only happen when you show focus, commitment, and passion.

As a reminder of how to deliver this style of leadership, in Figure 6.2 you will find an Equity Leadership Framework competencies document that recaps the skills covered in each of the five domains of the framework. Keep these competencies front and center to make certain your leadership efforts remain on track in bringing about equity.

Take Action—Now

Thank you for your leadership in becoming emboldened to confidently engage in an unconventional path toward equity that will shake the educational system at its very foundation. You're the right person for the job, and the time to act is now.

But before we part, let me leave you with the following thoughts:

Take the time to define and clarify equity.
Acknowledge negative conditions associated with race despite discomfort.
Keep working to build and support efficacy through intentional leadership.
Establish normalized actions around data and instruction that encourage an equity lens.

Accept the challenges of being an equity-driven leader.
Continue to keep in mind the definitive role you play in creating success.
Take steps that embolden a sense of purpose in those you lead.
Increase equity efforts through deliberate shared experiences.
Open an environment where all voices are solicited and heard.
Never forget that although times can be rough, *where all hope is lost, hope is found in you.*

Let the journey continue!

FIGURE 6.2

The Five Equity Leadership Framework Competencies

Define and Clarify Equity

The leader collaborates with staff to develop a working definition of equity that fosters an environment of disciplined people, thoughts, and actions.

Indicators

- Staff understand why equity is needed and can articulate a unified vision around equitable experiences for adults and students.
- Staff understand their responsibility and role in achieving equity.
- Staff can identify actions that support equitable experiences for adults and students.
- Staff's daily movements and actions align with the working definition of equity.
- A variety of data indicate that all students are getting what they need and are receiving open access to resources.
- Staff frequently revisit the working definition of equity and use it to monitor their thoughts and actions.

Create Discomfort

The leader sets the conditions for adults to have intentional dialogue conscious of race that challenges racial inequalities and deficit ideologies.

Indicators

- Adults have intentional space to reflect on their morals or values, experiences with race, and biases.
- Staff seek root causes of existing inequitable practices, thoughts, and actions implicated by race.
- The leader has clarity about existing collaborative supports and cooperative mindsets within the building and grasps where missteps might occur and to what degree conversations could constructively happen.
- Staff explore race from a variety of perspectives (personal, interpersonal, and global).
- Staff have collectively established conversation norms and ground rules.
- Staff regularly revisit conversation norms and ground rules, which are always front and center.
- Staff have deliberate opportunities to practice and reflect on active listening.
- Leadership facilitation of conversations shows an awareness of the racial dynamics in the room.
- Adults are action-oriented or function as educational equity allies, embracing differences, facing present realities, and rectifying circumstances dealing with injustice.

Build Efficacy

The leader positively influences the personal and collective belief systems of staff, building their capacity to deliver equitable outcomes.

Indicators

- The leader removes barriers that impede staff's ability to grow personally and professionally.
- The leader takes consistent action to gauge staff's levels of efficacy.
- There are no silos of teachers or staff in the environment.
- Staff are confident when facing challenges.

(continued)

FIGURE 6.2—(*continued*)
The Five Equity Leadership Framework Competencies

Build Efficacy—(*continued*)

The leader positively influences the personal and collective belief systems of staff, building their capacity to deliver equitable outcomes.

- Staff welcome collaborative practice and working together to solve complex problems about student learning.
- Staff can articulate how leadership and the common buildingwide goals support them in their work.
- Staff take on individual and collective accountability.
- Staff demonstrate persistence and resilience in meeting diverse needs (by setting challenging goals, making personal and teaching adjustments, and so on).
- Students believe that adults care for them.
- Staff hold high expectations for all students and keep their composure when supporting culturally diverse learners.
- Staff are willing to implement new ideas and strategies.
- The leader addresses deficit thoughts and behaviors by redirecting staff toward positive approaches and outlooks.
- The leader has established a culture that celebrates and recognizes quick wins.
- The leader is visibly and consistently present throughout the building.
- The leader solicits staff voices and empowers staff by sharing key responsibilities.
- The leader has arranged meaningful opportunities or structures for collaborative practice.
- The leader demonstrates situational awareness and fully understands the effect of their actions on staff.
- The leader offers staff a high level of care and support, accountability, and active engagement.
- The leader is collaborative and in tune with the thoughts and feelings of staff.

Normalize Action

The leader builds staff situational awareness by developing, monitoring, and strengthening an equity lens.

Indicators
- The leader has created a culture that routinely isolates race as a crucial factor to address.
- The leader has established a high level of trust among staff.
- The leader has fostered a culture of reflection in which staff exhibit self-governance and are aware of racially appropriate actions and conditions.
- The leader has established processes in which staff use data to disrupt systemic conditions by getting to root causes.
- Staff are committed to seeking out problems and establishing accountability measures to take ownership in creating change.
- The leader has created a culture in which staff seek out the stories of those marginalized to learn from them.
- Staff consistently collect and monitor data to understand the progress of day-to-day efforts.
- Staff identify solution-based outcomes that remove racial barriers and center on a multicultural perspective.

Normalize Action—(*continued*)
The leader builds staff situational awareness by developing, monitoring, and strengthening an equity lens.

- The leader consistently supports the development of an equity lens through classroom observations and coaching conversations.
- The leader monitors the learning environment to determine leadership's effectiveness in supporting staff.
- Staff are aware of practices that foster cultural connections.
- Staff can step outside themselves to identify the needs of learners with diverse backgrounds.
- The leader's approach to coaching thoughtfully navigates deeper discussion and reflection around race.

Leadership: Focus, Competence, and Passion
The leader exhibits focus, competence, and passion for motivating staff in creating an ecosystem centered around equity.

Indicators
- The leader frequently revisits the purpose of equity with staff to strengthen resilience and rejuvenation around the goal.
- The leader's words and actions align with the nature and scope of the work.
- The leader displays the obligation and desire to do what is right in the face of inequity.
- The leader focuses on the mission and stays at the forefront to engage stakeholders as crucial partners in the work.
- The leader establishes system structures and practices that promote constructive shared experiences.
- The leader seeks to understand perceptions of the current reality from all angles.
- The leader's disposition communicates a passion for developing people.

Acknowledgments

Leading Your School Toward Equity came to fruition through the assistance of many.

As a person of faith, I must first thank God, for it is by His grace that I was inspired to write the words in this book.

To my mother, Artis, and father, Edward, thank you for instilling in me the drive to do good in the world.

To my wife, Kanyon, you have certainly made my life better. Life is much easier when you find your best friend.

To my three children, Tia, Braylon, and Zevin, thank you for your unconditional love.

To my mother-in-law, Joceslyn, who encouraged me every step of the way during the writing process, I'm truly blessed to have received a mother-in-law as good as you.

And last but certainly not least, thank you to all the educators whom I have come across in my schooling and work. You have provided me the context and inspiration to fulfill this dream.

Appendix
A Toolkit for Active Equity Leadership

These tools are available for download at **www.ascd.org/EquityLeadership Toolkit**.

Tool A

Evidence Collection Form for a Leadership Climate Assessment

Collaborative Practice

Mindset

Reflective Practice

Culture

Tool B

Reflection Guide for Confronting Deficit Thinking

The issue we are currently grappling with is . . .	
Discovery Process	**Reframing Process**
Assessing	**Reassessing**
Examining Hidden Bias	**Building a Future State**

Write a reconstructed thought *(think proactive)* using the replacement words/thoughts.

Tool C

Planning Form for Equity Action Strategy Development

Gather: Data to review:

Gauge: What are we noticing about inequities?
1. 2. 3.

Grapple: How are we influencing the data?
1. 2. 3.

Glean: How will we elicit and learn from the voices that are missing from the table?
1. 2. 3.

Game Plan: Where do we go from here?	
What's working well: 1. 2. 3.	Ongoing challenges: 1. 2. 3.

What newly designed strategy or policy do we need to put in place to provide better support?

What will successful implementation look like from an equity perspective?

Tool D

Classroom Observation Guide for Culturally Responsive Strategies

Strategies Identified for Feedback:			

Planning for Success (before the lesson): **In the context of the lesson, what will successful execution look like from an equity perspective?**			
Desired Teacher Moves	1.	2.	3.
Desired Student Moves	1.	2.	3.

Culturally Responsive Strategies (during the lesson): **What did observers note about your use of culturally responsive strategies?**	
Record Teacher Moves	Record Student Response/Moves

Culturally Responsive Strategies (after the session): **What did observers notice about the students' level of engagement?**

Student Work (after the lesson): Assess samples of student work to discuss the effect of the strategy or strategies used. How did the strategy influence various learners?

Tool E

Guide to Culturally Responsive Strategy Patterns

Instructional Scale	
The overall teaching style communicates rigor. Observe what is happening in practice. More specifically, is there clear evidence that the priority is student learning, not adhering to pacing guidelines? Is the focus on lecturing or on purposefully seeking to engage and empower students during a learning period?	Scale ⟶ **High Pattern.** The teacher is exhibiting skill teaching all learners by navigating cultural barriers. The teacher shows an understanding of the different levels of access needed to ensure each student is invited into learning. **Some Pattern.** The teacher is showing skill teaching most learners. However, some students are not being reached. There is little to no observable pattern of racial inequity. **Low Pattern.** The teacher is not consistently showing skill teaching all learners. Racial inequity is apparent among those positively and negatively affected.
Learning goals communicate a higher standard of learning. Observe the intended purpose for learning. Does it set a high expectation? For example, does the purpose require students to engage in problem solving and critical thinking or just repeat information presented to them?	Scale ⟶ **High Pattern.** The lesson objective communicates a high expectation for learning. The outcomes are age appropriate and are aligned to stretch students' current abilities. **Some Pattern.** The lesson objective communicates a moderate expectation for learning. The outcomes may or may not be age appropriate, but they tend to reflect minimal advancement beyond students' current abilities. **Low Pattern.** The lesson objective communicates a lower expectation for learning. The outcomes are not age appropriate and merely maintain students' current ability.
Students are clear about their learning. Look for patterns of active student participation. Look for signs or indicators that all students are taking charge of their learning and can clearly articulate learning objectives. Can students show and explain what they were intended to learn?	Scale ⟶ **High Pattern.** All learners are working independently and are taking charge of their learning. When asked, they can both articulate and show deep comprehension of the task at hand and can connect to prior knowledge. **Some Pattern.** Many learners are working independently and are taking charge of their learning. When asked, most students can articulate and show comprehension of the task at hand. Few to no distinct patterns of racial inequity exist among those who are unclear about their learning. **Low Pattern.** There are clear signs of racial discrepancy among learners working independently and taking charge of their learning. Racial differences also exist among students who can articulate and show comprehension of the task at hand.

All learners are engaged in "good fit" activities. Look for good fit activities that provide students with the right level of challenge that doesn't lead to a high level of confusion or frustration.	Scale ⟶ **High Pattern.** All students are engaged in activities aligned with their current level of ability or understanding. Students are not easily working through tasks but experience deeper thought processes or challenges as they engage. **Some Pattern.** Most students are engaged in activities aligned with their current level of ability or understanding. Some students are engaged in lower-level activities, but few to no racial commonalities exist. **Low Pattern.** There are clear signs of racial discrepancy among those engaged in good fit activities, as opposed to those involved in lower-level activities.
Higher-level questions are appropriately leveraged for all learners. Look for questions that cover various depths of knowledge for multiple learners. Higher-level thinking questions are important for all learners, but they should be leveraged in a way that keeps all students invested in learning.	Scale ⟶ **High Pattern.** Higher-level questions promote inclusion of all learners. The teacher doesn't overuse higher depths of knowledge questions, leading to frustration, or underuse them, leading to student apathy. **Some Pattern.** The teacher asks higher-level questions, but students could benefit from more variety. The teacher may single out learners who are frustrated or apathetic, but there are few to no signs of racial commonalities. **Low Pattern.** The teacher sometimes asks higher-level questions and rarely varies them. The teacher tends to single out learners based on ability. There are clear indications of racial disparities among those who are appropriately engaged with questions or are challenged to think critically.
Emotional Resilience Scale	
Students are expected to participate and engage in learning. Look for persistence in ensuring that no students are permitted to opt out of learning. Watch for strategies and approaches that seek to build student resilience in sticking with challenges and problems.	Scale ⟶ **High Pattern.** All students are called to task and are expected to learn. The teacher encourages all learners to keep trying and work through perceived challenges. Scaffolded support is used appropriately in nudging students along (without taking away the responsibility for learning). **Some Pattern.** Most students are called to task and are expected to learn. However, some students are encouraged to keep trying and work through perceived challenges more than others, and not all are receiving the appropriate scaffolded support. Few to no racial commonalities exist among those not receiving support. **Low Pattern.** There are clear signs of racial disparities among those who are expected to participate and those who are permitted to opt out.

(continued)

Tool E

Guide to Culturally Responsive Strategy Patterns—(*continued*)

Emotional Resilience Scale—(*continued*)	
Students are given time to process and think. Look for opportunities where students are afforded appropriate wait time to gather their thoughts. This is crucial to building resilience.	Scale ⟶ **High Pattern.** All students are given the appropriate time to think and work through questions. The teacher not only uses wait time effectively for all students, but also does not allow students to be rushed or involuntarily bailed out by peers. **Some Pattern.** Most students are given the appropriate time to think and work through questions. The teacher tends to use wait time effectively for students, but allows some students to be rushed or involuntarily bailed out by peers. Few to no racial commonalities exist among those receiving inappropriate wait time. **Low Pattern.** There are clear signs of racial discrepancy among those who receive adequate wait time and those who are rushed or bailed out by the teacher or peers.
The teacher affirms and nurtures thinking as students seek solutions. Observe how the teacher is affirming student thinking or redirecting students as they provide and seek solutions. Positively supporting student thinking is important to build resiliency.	Scale ⟶ **High Pattern.** The teacher positively affirms all student thinking. The teacher encourages students to explore their thinking and appropriately corrects students' errored thinking. **Some Pattern.** The teacher positively affirms most student thinking. The teacher may not encourage some students to explore their thinking or may fail to appropriately correct students' errored thinking. Little to no racial commonalities exist among those whose thinking is not affirmed or nurtured. **Low Pattern.** There are clear signs of racial discrepancy among those who receive affirmation or nurturing of their thinking and those who do not.
The teacher provides immediate and timely feedback to students. Watch for feedback that is purposeful and that enables students to take advantage of the teachable moment. Timely feedback builds confidence in learning by giving students opportunities to make connections and adjustments in real time while learning is relevant.	Scale ⟶ **High Pattern.** The teacher observes students while they work and learn, seeking opportune times to support learning through feedback. The teacher consistently provides all students with immediate and timely feedback. **Some Pattern.** The teacher spends some time observing students while they work. The teacher consistently provides immediate and timely feedback to most students. Few to no racial commonalities exist among those who receive delayed or no feedback. **Low Pattern.** There are clear signs of racial discrepancy among those who receive immediate and timely feedback and those who do not.

The teacher provides specific feedback to students. Look for opportunities where learners can receive specific feedback to use and act on. Receiving and using feedback build resilience by helping students understand how to navigate both strengths and weaknesses.	Scale ⟶ **High Pattern.** The teacher observes students while they work and learn, seeking opportune times to support learning through providing specific feedback. The teacher consistently provides all students with specific feedback for them to act on. **Some Pattern.** The teacher spends some time observing students while they work. The teacher consistently provides specific feedback to most students. Few to no racial commonalities exist among those who receive generic or unspecific feedback. **Low Pattern.** There are clear signs of racial discrepancy among those who receive quality feedback and those who do not.
Environmental Scale	
The classroom is strategically arranged to promote a sense of equity. Does the classroom arrangement encourage student collaboration? Does the teacher ensure that seating assignments don't reflect students' learning abilities?	Scale ⟶ **High Pattern.** The classroom is arranged so that students can easily collaborate in small groups or pairs. Students are not clustered together based on their learning abilities or race. **Some Pattern.** The classroom is arranged so that students can collaborate in small groups or pairs. However, the permanent seating reflects some patterns of identifiable ability grouping. Few to no racial implications exist with the seating pattern. **Low Pattern.** The classroom may or may not be arranged for collaboration. Student seating arrangements reflect learning abilities and racial discrepancies.
Students can see themselves in the learning environment (in books, materials, shared stories, etc.). Look for signs or indications that all cultures represented within the classroom are valued.	Scale ⟶ **High Pattern.** The classroom environment provides opportunities for all students to see themselves in books, materials, shared stories, etc. **Some Pattern.** The classroom environment provides opportunities for most students to see themselves in books, materials, shared stories, etc. **Low Pattern.** The classroom environment provides limited to no opportunities for all students to see themselves in books, materials, shared stories, etc.

(continued)

Tool E

Guide to Culturally Responsive Strategy Patterns—(*continued*)

Environmental Scale—(*continued*)	
The teacher consistently applies behavior expectations that are culturally responsive to learners. Look for rules and expectations that marginalize groups of students. Do behavior expectations honor all learners? Does the teacher set and apply rules and expectations in ways that set all students up for success?	Scale ⟶ **High Pattern.** Rules and expectations are written and established in a way that is inclusive of all learners. They are implemented fairly and according to the needs of individual students. **Some Pattern.** Rules and expectations are written and established in a way that includes most learners. A few inconsistencies exist in how they are implemented, and some individual student needs may not be met. Few to no racial commonalities exist among those whose needs are and are not being met. **Low Pattern.** Rules and expectations are written and established in a way that is not inclusive of several learners. Inconsistencies exist in how they are implemented, and individual student needs are not being met. Racial commonalities exist among those whose needs are and are not being met.
All students feel safe to ask questions and explore their knowledge. Look for evidence that indicates an established culture of risk taking and asking questions to expand knowledge. Does the environment invite all learners to take risks? Students must feel safe or comfortable within the classroom environment to maximize their learning.	Scale ⟶ **High Pattern.** All learners take risks. All learners ask questions when they are unsure or seek ways to showcase or explore their knowledge. **Some Pattern.** Most learners take risks. Some learners either don't ask questions when they are unsure or don't showcase or explore their knowledge. Few to no racial commonalities exist among those who are not taking risks by asking questions and those who are opting not to showcase or explore their learning. **Low Pattern.** Learners don't take risks. Several learners either don't ask questions when they are unsure or don't showcase or explore their knowledge. Racial commonalities exist among those who are not taking risks by asking questions and those who are opting not to showcase or explore their learning.

The classroom promotes and showcases a higher standard of academic learning. Look for a classroom environment that celebrates and promotes student work. Look for anchors and supports for quality work that facilitate a higher standard for learning.	Scale ⟶ **High Pattern.** The classroom environment celebrates and promotes the work product of a variety of students. Appropriate anchors and supports are easily accessible to students, facilitating a higher standard of academic learning. **Some Pattern.** The classroom environment celebrates and promotes the work product of students with some variety. Some anchors and supports are visible, but they are not easily accessible to all students. There are no identifiable racial trends among student work that is celebrated. **Low Pattern.** The classroom environment does not celebrate and promote the work product of a variety of students. If anchors and supports are visible, they are not easily accessible to students. Racial trends exist among student work that is celebrated and not celebrated.

Using your equity lens, define the common characteristics of the students who do and don't understand.

Tool F

"REFLECT" Planning and Notetaking Guide for Equity Coaching

Rationalize: What is the purpose for the feedback (keeping an eye on equity)?
Empathize: What do I need to self-monitor or do to communicate to the coachee a sense of compassion and a desire to work together?
Focus: How will I stay curious?
Learn: How can I be helpful?
Engage: How can I communicate in the most honest and accurate way?
Check: How will I ensure that we have established joint understanding?
Target: What do I believe are important takeaways? When will I follow up?

References

Alexander, M. (2012). *The new Jim Crow: Mass incarceration in the age of colorblindness.* New Press.

Ashton, P. T., & Webb, R. B. (1986). *Making a difference: Teachers' sense of efficacy and student achievement.* Longman.

Baldwin, J. (2011/1962). As much truth as one can bear. In R. Kenan (Ed.), *The cross of redemption: Uncollected writings* (pp. 34–42). Vintage Books. (Original work published 1962)

Bandura, A. (1997). *Self-efficacy: The exercise of control.* W. H. Freeman.

Blankstein, A. M. (2011). *The answer is in the room: How effective schools scale up student success.* Corwin.

Boysen, G. A. (2012). Teacher and student perceptions of microaggressions in college classrooms. *College Teaching, 60*(3), 122–129.

Byrk, A. S., Gomez, L. M., Grunow, A., & LeMahieu, P. G. (2015). *Learning to improve: How America's schools can get better at getting better.* Harvard Education Press.

Colan, L. J., & Davis-Colan, J. (2013). *Stick with it: Mastering the art of adherence.* McGraw-Hill.

Collier, M. D. (2005). An ethic of caring: The fuel for high teacher efficacy. *Urban Review: Issues and Ideas in Public Education, 37*(4), 351–359.

Collins, J. C. (2001). *Good to great: Why some companies make the leap...and others don't.* Harper Business.

Covey, S. R. (1989). *The 7 habits of highly effective people: Powerful lessons in personal change.* Simon & Schuster.

Delpit, L. (1995). *Other people's children: Cultural conflict in the classroom.* New Press.

Delpit, L. (2012). *Multiplication is for white people: Raising expectations for other people's children.* New Press.

Derrington, M., & Angelle, P. (2013). Teacher leadership and collective efficacy: Connections and links. *International Journal of Teacher Leadership, 4*(1), 1–13.

Edmonds, R. (1979, October). Effective schools for the urban poor. *Educational Leadership, 37*(1), 15–24.

Ferguson, A. (2000). *Bad boys: Public schools in the making of Black masculinity*. University of Michigan Press.

Fullan, M., & Quinn, J. (2016). *Coherence: The right drivers in action for schools, districts, and systems*. Corwin.

García, S., & Guerra, P. (2004). Deconstructing deficit thinking: Working with educators to create more equitable learning environments. *Education and Urban Society 36*(2), 150–168.

Gibbs, S., & Powell, B. (2011). Teacher efficacy and pupil behaviour: The structure of teachers' individual and collective beliefs and their relationship with numbers of pupils excluded from school. *British Journal of Educational Psychology, 82*(4), 564–584.

Goddard, R. D., Hoy, W. K., & Woolfolk Hoy, A. (2000). Collective teacher efficacy: Its meaning, measure, and impact on student achievement. *American Educational Research Journal, 37*(2), 479–507.

Green, T. F. (1985). The formation of conscience in an age of technology. *American Journal of Education, 94*(1), 1–32.

Gregory, A., Huang, F. L., Anyon, Y., Greer, E., & Downing, B. (2018). An examination of restorative interventions and racial equity in out-of-school suspensions. *School Psychology Review, 47*(2), 167–182.

Gutsche, J. (2015). *Better and faster: The proven path to unstoppable ideas*. Crown Business.

Hammond, Z. L. (2015). *Culturally responsive teaching and the brain*. Corwin.

Hargreaves, A., & Harris, A. (2015). High performance leadership in unusually challenging educational circumstances. *Eesti Haridusteaduste Ajakiri* [Estonian Journal of Education], *3*(1), 28–49. http://dx.doi.org/10.12697/eha.2015.3.1.02b

Hattie, J. (2012). *Visible learning for teachers: Maximizing impact on learning*. Routledge.

Haycock, K. (2001, March). Closing the achievement gap. *Educational Leadership, 58*(6) 6–11.

Heath, C., & Heath, D. (2010). *Switch: How to change things when change is hard*. Broadway Books.

Hollie, S. (2012). *Culturally and linguistically responsive teaching and learning: Classroom practices for student success*. Shell Education.

Hoy, W. K., Sweetland, S. R., & Smith, P. A. (2002). Toward an organizational model of achievement in high schools: The significance of collective efficacy. *Educational Administration Quarterly, 38*(1), 77–93.

Johnson, R. S. (2002). *Using data to close the achievement gap: How to measure equity in our schools*. Corwin.

Kafele, B. (2021). *The equity and social justice education 50: Questions for improving opportunities and outcomes for Black students*. ASCD.

Kegan, R., & Lahey, L. L. (2009). *Immunity to change: How to overcome it and unlock potential in yourself and your organization*. Harvard Business School Publishing.

Kendi, I. X. (2019). *How to be an antiracist*. One World.

Ladson-Billings, G., & Tate, W. F. (1995). Toward a critical race theory of education. *Teachers College Record, 97*(1), 47–68.

Lewis, T. (2012, March 6). Black students face more discipline, data suggests. *New York Times*. https://www.nytimes.com/2012/03/06/education/black-students-face-more-harsh-discipline-data-shows.html

National Center for Education Statistics. (2020). *Why teachers of color matter for students of color to succeed.* https://www.edutopia.org/video/why-teachers-color-matter-students-color-succeed

Pajares, M. F. (1992). Teachers' beliefs and educational research: Cleaning up a messy construct. *Review of Educational Research, 62*(3), 307–332.

Parish, R., & Arends, R. (1983, January). Why innovative programs are discontinued. *Educational Leadership, 40*(4), 62–65.

Parks, M., Solmon, M., & Lee, A. (2007). Understanding classroom teachers' perceptions of integrating physical activity: A collective efficacy perspective. *Journal of Research in Childhood Education, 21*(3), 316–328.

Parrett, W. H., & Budge, K. M. (2012). *Turning high-poverty schools into high-performing schools.* ASCD.

Pate, A. (2020). *The innocent classroom: Dismantling racial bias to support students of color.* ASCD.

Peterson, J. S. (1999). Gifted through whose cultural lens? An application of the postpositivistic mode of inquiry. *Journal for the Education of the Gifted, 22*(4), 354–383.

Pierce, C. (1970). Offensive mechanisms. In F. Barbour (Ed.), *In the Black seventies* (pp. 265–282). Porter Sargent.

Pollock, M. (2004). *Colormute: Race talk dilemmas in an American school.* Princeton University Press.

Radd, S. I., Generett, G. G., Gooden, M. A., & Theoharis, G. (2021). *Five practices for equity-focused leadership.* ASCD.

Rawls, J. (1971). *A theory of justice.* Harvard University Press.

Reardon, S. F. (2016). *School district socioeconomic status, race, and academic achievement.* Stanford University.

Reynolds, J., & Kendi, I. X. (2020). *Stamped: Racism, antiracism, and you.* Hachette Book Group.

Robinson, V. M. J., Loyd, C., & Rowe, K. (2008). The impact of leadership on student outcomes: An analysis of the differential effects of leadership types. *Educational Administration Quarterly, 44*(5), 635–674.

Rosenthal, R., & Jacobson, L. (1968). *Pygmalion in the classroom: Teacher expectation and pupils' intellectual development.* Holt, Rinehart, and Winston.

Ross, R. (2013). School climate and equity. In T. Dary & T. Pickeral (Eds.), *School climate practices for implementation and sustainability: A school climate practice brief* (pp. 39–42). National School Climate Center.

Safir, S. (2017). *The listening leader. Creating the conditions for equitable school transformation.* Wiley.

Schein, E. (1992). *Organizational culture and leadership.* Jossey-Bass.

Schmoker, M. (1996). *Results: The key to continuous school improvement.* ASCD.

Schmoker, M. (1999). *Results: The key to continuous school improvement* (2nd ed.). ASCD.

Schmoker, M. (2016). *Leading with focus: Evaluating the essentials for school and district improvement.* ASCD.

Scott, M. (2017). *Even on your worst day, you can be a student's best hope.* ASCD.

Singleton, G. E., & Linton, C. (2005). *Courageous conversations about race.* Corwin.

Smith, D., Frey, N., Pumpian, I., & Fisher, D. (2017). *Building equity: Policies and practices to empower all learners.* ASCD.

Suárez-Orozco, C., Casanova, S., Martin, M., Katisaficas, D., Cuellar, V., Dias, S., & Smith, N. (2015). Toxic rain in the classroom: Classroom interpersonal microaggressions. *Educational Researcher, 44*(3), 151–160.

Sue, D. W. (2010). *Microaggressions in everyday life: Race, gender, and sexual orientation.* Wiley.

Tarca, K. (2005). Colorblind in control: The risks of resisting difference amid demographic change. *Educational Studies, 38*(2), 99–120.

Tatum, B. D. (1997). *Why are all the Black kids sitting together in the cafeteria?: And other conversations about race.* Basic Books.

Tschannen-Moran, M., & Barr, M. (2004). Fostering student learning: The relationship of collective teacher efficacy and student achievement. *Leadership and Policy in Schools, 3*(3), 189–209.

Watzlawick, P., Weakland, J., & Fisch, R. (1974). *Change: Principles of problem formation and problem resolution.* Norton.

Weinstein, R. S. (2002). *Reaching higher: The power of expectations in schooling.* Harvard University Press.

Wiggins, G., & McTighe, J. (1998). *Understanding by design.* ASCD.

Xoofish. (2013, March 11). *Elon Musk interviewed by Chris Anderson, March 2013* [Video]. YouTube. https://www.youtube.com/watch?v=MOXv7iR1AJk

Zambo, R., & Zambo, D. (2008). The impact of professional development in mathematics on teachers' individual and collective efficacy: The stigma of underperforming. *Teacher Education Quarterly, 35*(1), 159–168.

Index

The letter *f* following a page locator denotes a figure.

About the Author

Dwayne Chism is the Dean of the School of Education at Peru State College in Peru, Nebraska. He supports equity work at the local, state, and national levels and also works to support the development of current and aspiring leaders of color across the country. Chism previously served as principal supervisor, principal, and teacher. He founded Shifting Perspectives, LLC in 2018 to help schools navigate diversity to create equitable conditions for learning.

Chism's academic background includes a bachelor's degree in elementary education, a master's degree in educational administration, and a doctorate in educational leadership, all from the University of Nebraska at Omaha, where he was also named a Distinguished Alumni. He is the author of two *Educational Leadership* articles, "Paving a Coherent Path to Equity" and "Excavating the Artifacts of Student Learning."

Related ASCD Resources: Equity and Equity Leadership

At the time of publication, the following resources were available (ASCD stock numbers in parentheses):

Aim High, Achieve More: How to Transform Urban Schools Through Fearless Leadership by Yvette Jackson and Veronica McDermott (#112015)

Becoming the Educator They Need: Strategies, Mindsets, and Beliefs for Supporting Male Black and Latino Students by Robert Jackson (#119010)

Building Equity: Policies and Practices to Empower All Learners by Dominique Smith, Nancy Frey, Ian Pumpian, and Douglas Fisher (# 117031)

Cultivating Joyful Learning Spaces for Black Girls: Insights into Interrupting School Pushout by Monique W. Morris (#121004)

Cultural Competence Now: 56 Exercises to Help Educators Understand and Challenge Bias, Racism, and Privilege by Vernita Mayfield (#118043)

Culture, Class, and Race: Constructive Conversations That Unite and Energize Your School and Community by Brenda CampbellJones, Shannon Keeny, and Franklin CampbellJones (#118010)

Equity in Data: A Framework for What Counts in Schools by Andrew Knips, Sonya Lopez, Michael Savoy, and Kendall LaPro (#122021)

The Equity & Social Justice Education 50: Critical Questions for Improving Opportunities and Outcomes for Black Students by Baruti K. Kafele (#121060)

Excellence Through Equity: Five Principles of Courageous Leadership to Guide Achievement for Every Student by Alan M. Blankstein and Pedro Noguera with Lorena Kelly (#116070)

Five Practices for Equity-Focused School Leadership by Sharon I. Radd, Gretchen Givens Generett, Mark Anthony Gooden, and George Theoharis (#120008)

The Innocent Classroom: Dismantling Racial Bias to Support Students of Color by Alexs Pate (#120025)

Teaching with Poverty and Equity in Mind: Succeed with the Students Who Need You Most by Eric Jensen (#120019)

Turning High-Poverty Schools into High-Performing Schools (2nd Ed.) by William H. Parrett & Kathleen M. Budge (#120031)

For up-to-date information about ASCD resources, go to www.ascd.org. You can search the complete archives of *Educational Leadership* at www.ascd.org/el and keep up with the latest ideas, news, and solutions on the ASCD Blog at www.ascd.org/blogs.

For more information, send an email to member@ascd.org; call 1-800-933-2723 or 703-578-9600; or send a fax to 703-575-5400.

THE WHOLE CHILD

The ASCD Whole Child approach is an effort to transition from a focus on narrowly defined academic achievement to one that promotes the long-term development and success of all children. Through this approach, ASCD supports educators, families, community members, and policymakers as they move from a vision about educating the whole child to sustainable, collaborative actions.

Leading Your School Toward Equity relates to the **safe, supported,** and **challenged** tenets.
For more about the ASCD Whole Child approach,
visit **www.ascd.org/wholechild.**

WHOLE CHILD
TENETS

1 HEALTHY
Each student enters school healthy and learns about and practices a healthy lifestyle.

2 SAFE
Each student learns in an environment that is physically and emotionally safe for students and adults.

3 ENGAGED
Each student is actively engaged in learning and is connected to the school and broader community.

4 SUPPORTED
Each student has access to personalized learning and is supported by qualified, caring adults.

5 CHALLENGED
Each student is challenged academically and prepared for success in college or further study and for employment and participation in a global environment.